Freedom or Imprisonment

Freedom or Imprisonment

– The Relationship Between Self, People and Drugs

Paul Bonham

THE CHOIR PRESS

First published in the United Kingdom in 2021 by
The Choir Press

ISBN 978-1-78963-252-1

Contents

Preface

I have always been interested in people and their relationships. From working in a prison, in schools, with young people on the street and in clubs; I have listened to the way they interact with each other.

Within the prison I was a drug worker, and saw how choices of relationship with people and/or drugs were made. The personalisation of the drug, be it a substance such as alcohol or diazepam, or an activity such as social media or gambling, made me consider the impact on the "self". The drug is part of the conversation in many environments, actively playing a role through engagement one-to-one, or within a group. The dynamics of relationships with people reacting differently (of any age), became a fascination.

This has led to a certain approach to drug workshops with students. The Relationship approach seeks to discuss how, being relational, we choose both people and drugs with whom to interact. A workshop environment provides a variety of views and opinions. I like to introduce into the environment a sense of how important relationships are to each of us. In addition, how we act and feel differently, when we choose to introduce drugs into our environment. How do we manage these relationships? How do we care for our self as we interact?

The following book explores many aspects of relationship, with shared experiences and challenging questions.

Introduction

Why look at relationships?

Do you feel freed up or imprisoned by the relationships in your life? During the pandemic we have each looked at the environments in which we live. Home, work and places of leisure, and the relationships we have within them. What do we see and how do we feel? What is important to us and our "self", the person that we are and are to others.

Many have experienced a time of reflection. We may have a new understanding of the importance of certain relationships, or maybe the unimportance of others. This is connected to a consideration of our wants and our needs as we see them.

In the first chapter of this book we will look at how we are relational beings. Throughout our life journey we engage with others – people, drugs, as well as maintaining a constant dialogue with ourselves. The relationships we seek provide care, love, learning; as well as social development, enjoyment, kindnesses, praise, and empathy. Through interactions we gain confidence and ability to express ourselves, our opinions and views on what we receive from others.

We will look at how each person will walk a different pathway and be shaped by their own environments. Each will proceed at a different pace, and as a result, any relationship will present challenge. This is why we entertain different types of relationships at different times in our lives.

The following chapters will define the various interactions we encounter along our pathways. We will explore what it means to be in a relationship, in terms of the way it makes us feel and then act.

Shared experience, as part of each chapter, will include my own experiences within a work context, be it within prison, school or on the street. In addition, I will include comments made by myself and others, that have a relevance to the subject matter. Dramas, which feature as part of workshops, that place people and a drug (played by students) within a scenario, allow us to see and hear the participation of the drug within the relationship with individuals and the group. (For clarity and further explanation, the definition of words marked with an asterisk in the text can be found in the glossary.)

Throughout the book we will observe social pressures upon each of us and the ways in which relationships can be affected. We will feature the relationship that most have with social media. This relationship will vary from person to person in terms of investment of time and management of engagement. Together we will explore these areas; this chapter will examine how many that use social media will develop the persona of a resident, where the natural state of being is to be connected. Alternatively, that of a visitor, where the natural state of being is to choose to connect.

We seek to develop an understanding of what a model relationship may look like. A chapter on role models adds the dimension of who we may follow, how we may act. We look at what may be the benefits or risks of doing so. We return to the family relationship, primary care-giver and cared-for, and introduce the notion of a family space. How relationships impact upon our mental health – our self, is the most important topic, and how we can maintain a healthy and balanced state of mind in the face of so much input and output in today's world.

Towards the end we draw conclusions and look ahead to where our pathway leads. Then, have you heard of "fight or flight" in terms of an inbred response to threat of danger? Well, what about "Fight, flight or film it" – a bonus chapter.

So, if you want to explore relationship and how it might define your identity, your freedom to express yourself and be confident in who you are, or alternatively, where you may feel imprisoned by your engagement with people, drugs or your self, then read on.

Questions that you have may include – "I feel overwhelmed by the incoming messages, am I benefiting or at risk?"

"Who is important to me? Is there another type of relationship that I am having that I'm not sure is good for me, or that I have control over?"

Within this book we will explore how we are affected, and how we affect others in relationships. Who calls the shots?, and how our choice of interaction enhances or threatens our self. How we feel can be determined by the guides in our life, the road we take and the company we keep. We will look at you and other people: care-givers, colleagues, peers, mates and, of course, the vast swathes with whom you are in contact on social media.

We will look at you and drugs. We are all in relationship; that is we use, or are active with various drugs. At this point we need to say that the definition of a drug is something that alters your state of mind. It can be addictive, but doesn't necessarily lead to difficult or dangerous outcomes. We will be looking at our different interactions with drinking, gambling, cannabis and prescribed drugs amongst others. For many, a drug can become a personal friend, one who offers a shoulder to cry on, a pick-me-up, a buzz, a shelter, or company. There are as many different interactions as there are relationships that develop. The phone and its uses – social media is an important relationship in many lives.

We will look at, probably, the most important aspect of relationship: the one you have with your self. This is a continual dialogue consisting of receiving information, assessing the content, contributing to a state of mind (feelings) and response. We are instinctual beings and our self is constructed through experiences and safeguarded by boundaries to keep us safe. If we feel threatened, how do we react, which relationships do we turn to?

Chapter One

We are Relational

From the moment we are born, we start a journey of discovery through relationships that enter our lives. We begin a journey along a pathway* that, initially, is dependent on others, but later interacts with more input. We have a natural instinct to seek the support and care to survive and thrive. As we journey we learn about the environment we are in, those that are around us and who we are. If fortunate, in the early part of that walk, we have love, shelter, warmth, and a sharing and caring that informs us.

The following paragraph is my first reflection on relationship scenarios encountered during my working life that have informed my sharing.

Shared experience*

When I speak to students, I ask them about their first relationships. They answer mother, father, siblings (or not), grandparents – but what's next? They will answer, friends, and we speak about how we are different from each other and we seek others for various reasons. We question what we do when we do not receive what we need?

It is suggested, from my time working in a prison in drug recovery, that if the love of a family and the provision of warmth and shelter were missing, that friends (other people) may not necessarily be the choice of a relationship. This is where companionship may take on other forms – the drug*.

There can be an assumption that our initial relationship meets all our needs at that early time of life. Furthermore, that as we grow our primary care-givers recognise how our needs change, and provide care in other ways. While listening to prisoners' descriptions of early life experiences, there was a sense of lack of respect for their carers (parent/s, teachers, authority figures). Often, they would share that the relationship that they were seeking, one of love, shelter, warmth, food and encouragement, was missing or in short supply. For them it was a case of lack of trust. We will talk about the importance of the role of primary care-giver further on.

At times you could see where the trust between child and parent/carer was compromised, through family breakdown, neglect and abuse, that decisions could be made to engage with others experiencing similar troubles. Many prisoners shared that it would be only a short step to, for example, alcohol, cannabis or ecstasy. If they could not rely on or trust to be cared for by their closest relationship, then relationship or companionship may come from a drug.

Early experiences can shape our thinking as we proceed along our pathway. We need to form relationships that provide for our needs at various points of our life. These are connected to age, and linked to the development of our self: our physical development, psychological progression through our communication skills and social skills through interaction.

Guidance

We will talk about other influences we may encounter along our pathway, later in the book.

If we continue to refer to a journey along a pathway, we can introduce the form of a guide or guides. We need reassurance especially early on where all we are seeing, hearing and experiencing is novel and our response is unclear. Parental love, in the form of nurture, caring, and unconditional love; teachers that encourage the development of the young child, are both companions as we progress. For as we travel along, we encounter more traffic* (company/influences and junctions) on the road/path. These are the choices that we face. We may also face a narrowing or a widening of the path – these are early indications of alternative courses of action around freedom*. We will be looking at the implications of the junctions, and the narrowing and widening of the pathway, on our relational self later in the book.

With reference to the guidance that we accept into our company, we learn from our natural instincts as relational human beings. We seek learning, reassurance, and love/belonging – we need to trust. Within this book we will explore the plethora of relationships that we interact with, or not, in our own environments. Who is our environment, what is our environment – is it giving or taking? Who calls the shots, and what does that relationship look like, to us and to others? Later in the book we look at the personalisation that we introduce to not only our friends, but also the characteristics of drugs (be they substance or activity, legal or illegal). We are relational; we personalise, developing relationships on those terms.

The pathway ahead

As we walk along the path and mature, we look into the distance. We are setting goals, aims in life to satisfy our self, affirming our identity and expressing who we are. Through our interactions, our debates both external and internal, we address the issues of freedom (expression of views, exerting our rights); simultaneously, we can be looking at conforming with the stated view. This is the essence of *Freedom or Imprisonment*, within the title of the book.

As we grow older and achieve certain status within our environment, there is a need to assess where we are and where we are heading. We may have formed relationships that have endowed us with confidence. However, at the same time, there may be a point at which that sense of achievement may require a more secure approach. We look at safeguarding our self, assessing our current status of relationships.

What do we really feel is socially acceptable? What is my guide telling me, and is what they are telling me comfortable or not? There are many variables* (influences) to manage, control, review in terms of our relationships; these include mood, belonging, love, comfort against discomfort, my power, my identity and a need for reassurance that I am doing the right thing.

> ### Shared experience
>
> My personal thoughts – who to trust? I trust to try and live through and by the Spirit of Jesus, the Holy Spirit; to try to nurture a love for my fellow man and put aside the variables. I fail, as do we all, but my guide has no agenda or bias, this reassures me.

How we feel

Ultimately each of us is seeking to nurture a self; a representation of "who I am" that we are comfortable with and expresses who we are, how we feel and contribute to those around us. We learn from our care-givers and this continues throughout our whole journey. The traffic we encounter may influence us or not. We may decide to stop, listen and change course taking on a different guide. We may stop, listen and move on – maybe not agreeing, or instinctively feeling insecure. Later in the book we will dissemble the traffic and look at how we relate to it.

Our instinct feels important in our decisions to relate to others. The role of the environment we grow up in – the people, places and activities/occurrences that happen, affect the way we feel and react. Continuity, at an impressionable age, within an environment sets strong foundations. This is important as you journey along your pathway. When we explore what freedom may look like, in terms of expression of your self and certainty of opinion; trusting our instinct and others we relate to within our environment is reassuring. What do we believe in, and what do we want to say? Is this how I feel and am I comfortable with this? Or am I captive to beliefs or statements of view that vary from my gut instinct? Has my self been compromised and how?

As we look further into relationships – how we construe them and how much we are influenced positively or negatively – we will recognise the changing pathway, its narrowing and widening, the traffic encountered and the variables that shape our thinking.

Summary

Each of us is individually shaped, in terms of the ways in which we react to input. Our mood, in so far as what we choose to share and with whom, and how much we listen and take things in. However, we are all similar in that we are relational. We receive and speak out through relationships formed within environments we live in.

We also live by instinct. Through our interaction, in early life, teenage and older years; we develop an instinct that expresses itself through who we are, how we are, what we do and why we do.

There are a number of guides that accompany us that relate to us in different ways – some primary, some secondary in nature. The environments we move through are situations; and within each, people, both single and in groups (even masses).

Our experiences, and our feelings through our self are affected by our relationships and in the situations we interact with them.

Questions

- Where do you seek and find safety and unconditional love today?
- Identify your environments, and key relationships – look at the balance (who calls the shots?).
- Do you see any relationships that are seen as socially acceptable, are you comfortable buying into this?
- Is your self represented in any, some, or all your relationships?

Journal

Chapter Two

Getting Personal With . . .

As we journey along our life's pathway, we will encounter others (people and drugs). Even if we consider ourselves solitary in our outlook, there will be company at the end of a phone, featured on a screen (image and voice), and an internal dialogue going on with ourselves. We are relational beings, we exchange information, receive and give within the environment we are in. This is how we develop our sense of ourselves and the environment we inhabit, and form an identity that represents us. We are never alone.

Shared experience

I recall that when I worked in prison, often someone might share that since they returned to imprisonment they had "now lost it all, everything". Later in the book we will explore imprisonment as part of a journey down a particular pathway. My response would be to allow the person to talk and express what they mean by "everything". I would hope that they would recognise that there was someone sitting opposite who was standing with them looking at the junction that they had reached.

A key feature of our relational aspect to others is our learning, acquiring and processing the input and forming the output; in other words, the response. This is shaped and influenced by the environment(s) we move into as we walk our pathway. Our social development is further developed by our secondary choices of company, people and/or drugs, after our primary care-givers. As we have already said, this is a junction* we arrive at, where our choice may differ according to our prior experience. If I choose to share and spend time with this person/drug, will I feel comfortable or uneasy – what does my instinct tell me? Our instinct develops as we walk along, influenced by the company we keep and interact with.

To underline the personalisation that occurs, we will look at a dialogue between two people around the choice of person or drug. The following dialogue seeks to show how two friends express their views on engagement with people and drugs. This is a drama used in workshops.

Shared experience

James – I am comfortable with relationships with people.

Stella – I am comfortable with relationships with drugs.

James – But you can't have a conversation.

Stella – One of my best mates (alcohol) is down the pub.

James – I get it, a beer/wine, but they can let you down.

Stella – No problem. If I feel fed up, a bit down, I've got pills for that and they are not drugs.

James – You can't fix everything with drugs, and prescribed pills are drugs anyway. It's best to talk with family or friends.

Stella –That's all fine, but you know how relationships can go wrong with people.

James – True, both people and drugs. Why do you think that some choose one and some the other?

Stella – I am not always comfortable with people face to face, saying something I don't like, making me feel rubbish; drugs can't talk, don't look at you and don't judge!

James – Didn't you say you had a mate down the pub? But I agree with you, why do you think sometimes people choose both, and it's not always a bad thing?

Stella – Sometimes people can make you feel good or bad, just like drugs. Why?

James – Well, for me it's about me as an individual. Just take you, we are different: different personality, different background, different moods and different choices.

Stella – That's the point – we have a choice. If I think about it, I choose to use drugs – prescribed, legal, sometimes illegal.

James – Yeah, and don't forget that phone of yours, if anyone was ever addicted to something you are! So am I, a drug can be an activity that alters your state of mind – you know what I'm like when I start gambling.

Stella – Don't be too hard on yourself. Most of us spend a lot of time doing these things, smoking, drinking – but they're not necessarily bad for us.

> **James** – It's about moderation, managing the drug/relationship; we have both known mates that have lost that control, and the drugs used them. If I'm honest I get desperate if my battery's low, and I can't help playing another hand if I'm losing.
>
> **Stella** – None of us is perfect, but that's where I reckon we need people; they see us, sense how we are, see things are getting out of hand. Thanks, mate!
>
> **James** – Cheers, pal. See you down the pub!

What perspective do you tend towards? They are friends, know each other well; it's a relationship where differences of opinion and alternative views are accepted. They appear to be people with experience of relationships with both people and drugs.

Given that their chat includes interaction with friends, social media, alcohol, gambling, prescribed and illegal drugs; many of us could actually step into one or both roles. You may be able to replace a drug with another but it is clear from the way the conversation goes, that interaction with both people and drugs is normal.

The fact that the two are, by all accounts, friends and know of the relationships each has and are comfortable sharing, suggests that they see the drug and the person as accepted personal relationships. However, when talking about the word "drug", a different sense can arise. Different people have different perceptions; some will see a drug from a personal perspective, others may consider a drug from what has been said in various media.

Shared experience

When in a workshop, I would display an array of drugs on a table (some would not be real, but appear so – cocaine and heroin). In addition, a phone, game controller, prescribed pills like codeine and temazepam, alcohol, cannabis, playing cards, and a magazine in a brown wrapper (pornography).

Students (aged eleven to eighteen), would be invited to select the most dangerous to them. Most would choose heroin, probably the next choice would be the phone. When I asked when they had last used heroin, and how much, they denied it and we spoke about how it was based on perception not experience. Those who chose the phone shared how they knew someone who had experienced problems to varying degrees.

You will make choices about using/interacting with others dependent on a whole range of factors: the company that you are in; how you feel; experiences in the past (personally or known through others); through age, and you can add many more. The choice of a relationship with another person will also be affected by similar thoughts.

There are certain associations that "getting personal with", because of the perceived nature of the "other", may see you move into an environment that is uncomfortable for some. It happens when the other is possibly (perceptions differ) socially unacceptable. Quite often this judgement is open to debate, as each of us is different. The company within the environment may collude and invite others to ratify use or association.

Relationships are formed with drugs that many describe as socially acceptable; alcohol is the obvious one. Many people would not accept that it is a drug, because their sense of the word drug suggests negative effects (harm), possibly illegality. As we have already discussed, a drug is something that alters your state of mind. This alteration can impact differently on different people.

Interaction with social media is fed by the fact that so many people are interacting. You can see from the conversation within the drama earlier on, that there is a suggestion that one of them cannot manage the relationship. We will see later in the book that many people reside on social media, in that it is their natural state and where they reside and interact. The conversation acknowledges through the dialogue that each of us engages with both people and drugs. In addition the relationship can endure ups and downs, and that these changes originate from the person.

We will look at the input and output from the drugs perspective later in the book through an exercise. This exercise (in the next chapter), played out within a workshop by students playing an interviewer, a person in a relationship with a drug, and a drug itself, demonstrates the way each looks at how their relationship has developed.

The conversation also demonstrates the benefit of a friend – someone who has your best interests at heart. There is a space for sharing, a trust and a desire to support one another. In terms of freedom of the individual, we see opportunity to express oneself and by listening, to learn from others. Who are your friends?

We can see from this dialogue that the relationships discussed offer similar experiences. There is an acknowledgement that people and drugs (substances, activities including gambling, social media, gaming, and others), can appear personalised. We do this to normalise interaction with the company.

Shared experience

> I often heard, in the prison, "It's socially acceptable, isn't it?" – when referring to drinking, gambling, or snorting a drug.

We will all have relationships with both people and drugs. What type of relationships are they? As we journey down our pathway, we encounter different company as we enter different environments. We identify with others according to how we perceive what we need at that time in our journey. Thus, your primary care-givers (family, carer, teacher, health providers) may satisfy a need to belong, to be loved, to provide a foundation/base, shelter, safety, for example. However, they may not; we all take different paths, and as a result, encounter different company at different times of our lives, not always a positive experience.

We have a desire to establish an identity – this is who I am. This is what I look like, my image; this is what I believe in or represent. Sometimes, this image can be impacted upon by the other in our chosen relationship, be they person or drug. Each individual displays certain characteristics, moulded from their journey, that can reveal a leader or a follower, or somewhere in between. The leader within us may show characteristics of pushing the boundaries, exploring new ways of looking at life and presenting a different image than the norm. The follower may, through a sense of security, belonging, fitting in, tend towards choosing company that appears to attract the majority.

When we are talking about variables that exist and colour our thinking about relationships, we will all experience certain feelings that are commonplace. These feelings will naturally include those such as sexual instincts, envy, greed and exerting power over others. These influences on our thinking may affect the nature of any relationship, be it with person or drug.

Shared experience

When in the prison, someone shared that the first time he used cocaine with alcohol in a pub/bar, was like seeing a woman and falling for her immediately. He couldn't wait to see her again, and again. Another example given was with gambling, and the desire to win that big life-changing amount; the power of the other (cards, online gambling, horses, dogs, etc.) making me careless of anyone/anything else.

Further, in terms of aspects of company that we encounter within our environments, peer pressure – the imposing of another's preferences on our own in terms of choices, will affect the relationship choices we make. This variable can influence our feelings of freedom or imprisonment in relation to our identity and expression of our self. We will talk later in the book about the shifting balance of relationships and how they impact on the self within different environments.

When we assign personality to the drug as well as to the person within a relationship, then we see a recognisable setting (as relational beings) for giving and receiving. For example, you may choose to enter a relationship with alcohol because of enjoyment, to change mood, you enjoy the taste, or because people you know drink. In return, alcohol will give enjoyment, alter your mood, and satisfy. How long the relationship continues in the same way will differ from one individual to another. The relationship will change because the person will change; have the reasons for the choice altered, why and is the user still benefiting or not? This review is a constant as environments change, people change, and the company change as they travel along the pathway.

Summary

We all experience relationships with people and drugs; in addition, we constantly converse with our self. The way we feel, the moods that we experience are the response we have from the self.

Our learning, acquiring and processing of input forms our response: and how we are experienced by others, those that we are in relation with. Importantly, both people and drugs respond in kind.

As a result of interaction with company, we form an identity. This can also be described as "image"; how we are perceived in society and as part of society. Through the dramas we can see how, through interaction, we adopt a stance, a look; this is also seen through our instinct as a leader or a follower.

Each of us seeks different things at different times along our pathways. Generally, there are common drivers – belonging, to be loved, to love, greed, power and learning (experiences) are examples.

Questions

- Can you recall any particular relationships (person or drug) that have shaped you today?
- Are there different types of relationships within your different environments? What do they contribute?
- Leader or follower? How does this demonstrate itself?
- Have you identified peer pressure in an environment that has impacted on your self?

Journal

Chapter Three

Person, Drug or . . .

We have seen how each of us, as human beings, journeys along a path that is unique. It is defined by the relationships that we automatically experience within environments that we inhabit. Along that pathway we arrive at junctions, where we make choices on further relationships; based on instinct, mood, desire to learn and express oneself, to belong, to love and share with others. This is not an exhaustive list and, as we have seen, a number of variables impact on our reasoning as well.

We are experiencing growth – physically, socially, emotionally – and forming a self that we wish to represent who we are. Each individual has a need for empowerment, a feeling of comfort and reassurance; we are requiring interaction and collaboration from others in our environment to achieve.

Though people are similar, in that they seek relationships for reasons that align, we are on different journeys. Our early influences will differ and our development will vary in the areas mentioned. In this way, we can see that the needs from the other, within a relationship, may match – such as things in common, similar outlooks, shared opinions, but ourselves and the other may be arriving at the relationship from a different base-point. An example might be illustrated in a drama, within a workshop that I deliver, around two friends who, at the end of a week, can't wait to meet at a party to drink/socialise.

Shared experience

Scene: a party.

Alcohol – Great party! Always is when I am around and I am always around. Thing is, I appeal to most people – celebrating or commiserating. I am your man/woman!

Sam – Hi, Jack. I knew there would be some booze, always is at Zara's. Do you know what? I fancy my chances with Zara, but will probably need a few first.

Jack – Well, I am going to join you in a few beers. But for me it's to forget last week, wipe it out, my parents arguing again – and I am the one caught in the middle.

Alcohol – So we are all best mates, but not sure these two are going to end up with what they want, when I take control.

Later ...

Sam – Hi, Zara. It's me, Sam. I've always liked you; do you want a drink?

Zara – No thanks. How's Jack? Looks like he's fed up, and this flat is running out of beers!

Sam – Look I will get you a drink, and we can talk somewhere.

Zara – You are being pushy, go and see how Jack is and see if he's noticed me.

Alcohol – Can you see how I'm involved here?

Later ...

Sam – So, feeling better? Zara's complained that you are drinking far more than you brought to the party, and you are getting in the way of Zara and me.

Jack – I think that if you believe you have a chance with her, you've had too many! Leave me alone!

Alcohol – It's not quite working out for either of them. Funny how the mood changed. Anyway I've had a great time, I am, after all, socially acceptable!

Sam has had a really good week, and sees a drink as a way to celebrate, enhance the good mood. Jack has experienced a bad week, he see a drink as something that will alter his mood and help him feel better. As it turns out, neither is satisfied and argue; the point is that the two are inviting a third (alcohol) into the relationship from a different perspective.

We see an agenda brought to the situation by each of the company. The people involved contribute to the general conversation and we, as observers, can see what their intentions are. Is alcohol an observer or a participant? As we hear from each participant, we notice a control trying to be exerted within the environment. This is where the agenda is revealed. As this becomes clear to the other, there is a reaction, based on their own narrative.

Alcohol is interacting and its participation can alter the mood. In itself alcohol – you may substitute it for another drug – is another that exists to serve needs in an environment.

How well do we know the other?

If someone, as we have already explored, portrays in company a side of themselves that does not represent their real self, then the interaction suddenly looks more complicated; outcomes can be unpredictable. The same consideration of "who are they?", can be applied to the drug. We hear the term "recreational drug" applied to certain substances (alcohol, cannabis, ecstasy, for example), referring to common (accepted) use that may be considered enjoyable and relaxing. The question is, of course, who is saying this, is it really the reality of their use and would it necessarily apply to my use? The drug does not alter from a description of recreational to harmful; it is our response to our interaction with it and the impact of the company we are in.

The space we engage with each other in, can expand or feel closed in sometimes when in company. Why is this? We are different people, in different places, at different times. Our state of mind is fluid and our mood changes, as we experience an environment.

It may be helpful to look at some examples. Many of us have a relationship with keeping fit, with a gymnasium as the environment. People arrive with differing reasons to be there, from starting out with little or no experience, to competing against targets (or maybe other people), or a social interaction. There may be a range of purposes together. In addition, because it is a place where people can be comparing/competing with others, the way we feel, and how we engage/respond can be represented in different ways. As we revisit the environment, we can appear to change altered by our interaction not only with others, but seeing the nature of the environment differently.

Has it ever been the case that someone outside that environment has mentioned a difference not only physically, but in what you're like? They may not know the environment, so part of their thinking will be based on not knowing it themselves.

You can probably think of other examples, such as a compulsion to gamble online, residing on social media, or indulging in pornography, where a person seems to live differently in different spaces. Clearly the relationship, that they have cultivated, may be in an environment that can be addictive for any number of reasons.

Each of us has boundaries that we need to be in place when in new company, with a person or drug. We want to be comfortable and safe. This foundation allows us to express ourselves and to feel a sense of freedom. However, when the dynamics change within the environment the boundaries shift.

We are investing something of ourselves in relationships to varying degrees; at some point, there needs to be a trust that the interaction is with the real self of the other. We will be looking later in the book, at how we can feel obliged to adopt a persona that is not reflective of our self in order to fit in or belong.

As we have already spoken about we form relationships with people and drugs, as we encounter different company in different environments, in different mindsets. I always emphasise, when talking in workshops, that the word drug in terms of a relationship partner, can influence us positively and negatively regarding physical and mental health based on a number of variables, which we will look at later in the book. The drug will offer something in terms of the relationship. It may be a large part of your life, in which you invest a lot of time, energy, and importance. Alternatively, a relationship that we can engage with or do without, with ease. Sometimes the use of a recreational drug may be viewed like this. However, we need to reiterate how this can be misleading: we are all different and our responses are as well.

The relationship with a drug, on many occasions, introduces an element of a personality that we engage with: an example may be a prescribed medication that can develop into a dependent partner such as diazepam. Many will be aware of the term "Mother's little helper".

Shared experience

When in the prison, many people came in that were climbing the walls, not because of an addiction to an illegal drug, but to a legal prescribed medication (probably obtained on the street). Another example might be, where a relationship had been formed with bodybuilding/gym attendance to the extent that steroids had become the dependent partner. The environment and the company have colluded to make the drug-use an acceptable and controlled activity.

Thus, the drug may become more than a friend, and present as an activity or a substance, that can to others be merely a pastime or interest.

The factors that impact on the balance within the relationships originate from the person in this type of relationship. The variables that we have discussed influence the way we interact: mood, others in an environment and what we are receiving/giving. Over time these factors alter the nature of the person-to-drug relationship. These examples will explain further the shifts that take place.

Shared experience

I sat down with a prisoner whose relationship with a drug(s) had led to his crime. In order to gauge the relationship, I asked, "When did you last use cocaine?"

He replied, "I think it was a couple of nights ago, but not sure – lost track of time."

I said, "Did you use it?"

"Yes, didn't you hear me?"

I said, "Or did it use you?"

I wasn't interested so much in the timeline, but when the relationship fundamentally changed in terms of boundaries, safety, control and, therefore, the mood and status of the drug.

The second example, within a workshop, explores the way in which both the person and drug look at the relationship. A third party asks the questions of each (within the workshop, a student takes the part of a drug chosen by the "person" – included are the typical answers).

Shared experience

Interviewer – Why did you choose the relationship?

Person – My friends are doing it, need cheering up, something to do, curious.

Drug – I didn't.

Interviewer – You have been together for a while, how is it going?

Person – Mostly what I expected, enjoying my time.

Drug – I have lots of relationships like this; I'm available whenever.

Interviewer – Who calls the shots?

Person – Well, I do, when I want to use, play; it's up to me.

Drug – He/she does.

Interviewer – How does your relationship affect other relationships?

Person – Not sure, you would have to ask them. I have got other friends. But naturally, I spend more time with drug.

Drug – There is plenty of me to go round; the more the better.

Interviewer – How is knowing each other going to help your future?

Person– Not sure, I am thinking that it depends on how much time will be taken up by my job, education and how that fits with other relationships. I might have to make commitments that could be affected.

Drug – I would want our relationship to continue and maybe become more involved. I don't have any other considerations.

Interviewer – What would make you end the relationship; could you?

Person – I suppose that if it didn't fit with everything else, or I was not enjoying it as much. But other people I know use/play and they are OK, but maybe I wouldn't know if they weren't.

Drug – It's not up to me.

To summarise this interview, it is a relationship where there is an interaction going on between person and drug. The main driver appears to be the person; as the drug, in substance or activity form, cannot initiate conversation and show feelings or demonstrate moods. The relationship can produce enjoyment/pleasure for the person, but also prompt questions in the mind of the user. The drug, on the other hand, is used.

We can observe a change in the balance and investment from the person; only the person will feel it and, dependent on the nature of the relationship and the environment that they inhabit (influence of others, people and drugs), may not disclose problems to others or themselves.

We have explored the nature of the person-to-drug relationship. Importantly, an internal relationship, that with oneself, is a continuous dialogue that we need to consider. We need to understand how our relationship with our self develops, changes and safeguard ourselves. What defines me, and how do I appear to others? Do I feel I am growing in understanding, and establishing an identity that I am happy with and trust? Is the company about me that I relate to, positive and encouraging and helping to shape a self that I recognise, and not an image of someone else that I would be uncomfortable to know?

We will look later in the book at mass input from multiple platforms, as we move along our pathway into many environments that influence our daily lives.

To me, we need a simplification as to the guiding relationships that we encourage. The relationship with our self is the most important. This relationship determines our moods, well-being, personal growth leading towards increased confidence and self-assurance. We benefit from relationships that are giving, sharing, and adopt the role of a listener when needed. Our self is nurtured by others in our company that are invested in the relationship without outside interference.

As a relationship grows in value, a reliability or dependency can develop. The other person or people in a group should recognise this and honour this investment. This is where, when in the traffic of company, a careless remark may be shared that can damage. The various modes of communication from verbal (present or not), messaging of many types within the relationship, can be misconstrued. Our choice of company and participation needs to be conscious of a need to safeguard the self. Where we have the person-to-drug relationship, or where the drug is part, the drug does not assess, or alter in nature to changes in the relationship. Being the "used" it only affects, but remains unaffected. Therefore, the person has the responsibility to adjust if needed – to spend less time with, accord less importance to, or finish it.

The self of the user can be vulnerable to how a relationship affects their mood, safety and insecurity as it continues and develops, with person or drug.

Summary

As relationships occur, we have to be aware that we and the other, or others, will be coming from different starting points. As individuals, the drivers for the relationship will range from a need to alter a mood to a desire to be needed.

When we are in the relationship, to a certain degree, we are exposing ourselves to another. That other person we may not even see or be with, and a trust may be required as the relationship develops. Each of us needs to observe the dialogue, check in with ourselves; in other words, review what we are saying and what we are being told.

The importance of review, when in relationship, safeguards against potential mental-health concerns. We should seek simplification; identify relationships that we have a clear understanding of, and where our needs are met.

Questions

- Does the environment that you inhabit affect the person that you are, and that appears to others?
- It might be useful to answer the interview questions from this chapter, for you and a chosen drug.
- Ask a friend if and how you change when drinking, using cannabis or gaming for example. How?
- Do you safeguard your self when using social media, e.g. feel pressurised or threatened, regretting a post, maybe an image that is out there?

Journal

Chapter Four

Imprisoned?

We have seen how the development of relationships, as part of the growing process of each of us, can contribute to making our way towards goals and ambitions. What we could perceive as freedom: the power or right to the expression of thoughts, opinions – our positioning with society. Our self gaining in confidence, security and reassurance.

As we experience this change, through the company we seek from the traffic on our pathway, there will surface certain feelings of doubt, concern or worry about these steps forward. This is only natural, as we know in ourselves that we have boundaries of safety that are instinctual, and that trust is not a given, either way, at first.

New environments

The expansion of our contact list and encountering of new relationships in new environments can introduce doubt. There are many examples of where change can make us hesitate. We can move area, adopt new family, change school/work, or try a new leisure activity. Certainly, the phase of our growth and development as an individual will have a bearing on how we adapt. At the same time, reassurance from care-givers at home or elsewhere, will maintain some consistency in our lives.

The benefit of listening from guides is imperative. We all need to be able to express our feelings and this is difficult to contemplate with new company in new environments. It may have been the case that we had been moving forward with confidence and a certain freedom. When we face change, it is important that we can stabilise our situation; ideally not taking a step back. The space that we live in can feel different, uncertain. This is where an empathic approach can be valuable in resetting oneself.

This reset* is the "pulling over" to take time for a conversation with ourself. It is at this time that we can review our support mechanisms, those foundational relationships, and develop plans for the road ahead. In general, each of us seeks a balance within our environments and with the company there. In order to safeguard ourselves we desire to manage our relationships. As people that are developing their sense of self, there needs to be challenge to learn and step up. At the same time, depending on our personality, we have a sense of reassurance from conforming to the views of like-minded people. There is a certain reassurance in conforming within society as we travel along our pathways in our choices. There is a balance to be found for each of us.

This is the juxtaposition between freedom and imprisonment in the sense that stepping out (into new environments) and remaining behind bars (security of what is known) is a continuous fact of daily living. It is seeking, for most of us, the balance that suits us.

Shared experience

Within the prison system there exists a community. The community is made up of officers, inmates and civilians. Each wing houses a population where there is an understanding that there are boundaries. In order to live alongside each other, the prison seek agreement to acknowledge and live by the rules and to be productive – work and education (rehabilitation). To give structure, understood by all in the community, there are regimes whereby inmates are allowed or disallowed certain privileges. There is association where they can meet others, and have the opportunity to form relationships and also recreation.

Pulling over

Those convicted are removed from society, in order to address the harm that they have imposed; harm that, through offending, they will have imposed on themselves. The imprisonment intends to safeguard, introduce a period of stability and an opportunity for a reset.

In terms of the personal journey, it is a pulling over, albeit enforced. They were travelling in a direction in the company of certain traffic, where influences may have been negative (however it started out). The prison is a primary care-giver. In essence it provides shelter, nourishment, support (sometimes not accepted, or seen as such), isolation if needed, or association, and a way forward (again, if chosen or accepted). The opportunity may be there, depending on the individual, to consider/reconsider their secondary relationships.

The regime of the prison, through necessity, has a structure; from the foundation, which are the rules to a way forward. The inmates are all in different places. In comparison to their most recent experiences, and choices of relationships and environments, there may be a place of safety. Certainly, this isn't always evident in their attitude, but inside it may be felt. For others, the imprisonment has prevented them from pursuing a lifestyle that, on the face of it, they profit from, but on reflection may have repercussions for themselves and others they know.

Many consider imprisonment as an impediment to progressing with a lifestyle outside. However, they may also use the time to assess the road ahead, in terms of real gains and what their freedom is costing. When comparing the nature of the environment inside: the regime, the structure of work, association, support and education, with a lifestyle outside – how does it look? Of course, roles are played out within prison, but are they not also played out similarly outside?

This scenario of imprisonment seeks to explore the way in which we can withdraw (forced or otherwise), when necessary, to take stock. The relationships that we choose to participate in, sometimes by design, other times through environmental influences, sometimes run away with us. It can be useful to apply the brake, step away and look at the interaction from outside. Freedom, in terms of self-advancement is beneficial and moves us down the road. However, how are we appearing to others? Do we appear as someone we would be happy to know, listening and encouraging, with sound foundations?

As we have mentioned previously, there is temptation to choose people or drugs. We have to remind ourselves that, within society, the relationships we choose (and we do choose both) we need to nurture, manage through self-assessment using our instincts (our self), and seeking support that is empathic and coming from a neutral standpoint. This is especially important where the individual, at any given time, has a propensity to over-indulge, over-invest in the relationship, in a desire to change their mood. We have seen this previously through the characters, both people and drugs, involved in the dramas and interviews in prison.

The prison environment presents an isolation, through captivity, as well as the option of different company within the community of a prison. The choice is that of the inmates – should they use the pulling over enforced upon them to reset themselves? Should they take the opportunity, without the usual traffic around, to reflect, listen to his/her self without outside interferences?

Shared experience

When I was in the prison, I would sit down and ask my client to tell me about the situation. Many said that it was the first time for some time, that they had an opportunity to talk and be heard. It was encouraging to talk to themselves, and importantly, to listen to how they feel. To be able to cut out the static of mass input and check in with your self is to care for yourself. Quite often they lived hectic lives, running around meeting demands made by others and having no time to listen to themselves.

Self-management

Empathy is important. This approach can be seen as standing at the hole that someone is in, and being present, but *not* jumping in it to join the person needing support. The best outcome is where your guide walks alongside, encouraging you to develop your own recovery plans. The internal dialogue that the inmate has may resemble a conversation including: what were my plans, is my destination any nearer, how far have I come, what has worked, what hasn't? In addition, looking outside your self, which relationships within the environments I live are healthy, which are damaging – even toxic – and that includes people and substances and activities.

There is a sense that the freedom we look for, within the environments in which we live out our daily lives, is more accessible today. The range and type of relationships where we can exercise our rights to voice opinions is limitless.

It is important to note that we have to be aware that there are individuals that are especially vulnerable; those who are young, of an age where they can be vulnerable, and those that find it difficult to cope with the static of modern society through mental-health challenges. As individuals we are all presented with different challenges to deal with as we live out our daily lives.

Within the busy environments that we occupy, is how we come across to others a representation of "I" or "we"? Whose views are being declared and to whom or how many? The relationships that we participate in are external, but they also impact upon our self. We need to be aware of a conditioning that can alter the way we represent ourselves. The follower, and most of us are, will move with the popular view. This does not mean that we are not advancing down our pathway towards our goals. There is a certain reinforcement from being one of a number. The leader may step out in another direction. They may adopt a direction because their instinct (gut feeling) is telling them something else. Of course, things change and in a different situation, another may step out strongly themselves for the same reasons.

The prison, as a symbol of captivity, provides an example of how a regime may facilitate a personal review of environment and relationships within it. At some point, we may need to impose constraints upon ourselves, in order to safeguard the person that we are.

We need to ensure that we don't lose our initial reasoning for developing associations with people and drugs. How a relationship is going to improve me. We are always learning, developing interests that give us confidence, and sharing in healthy activity and conversation. This enhances our sense of self. It is about being patient, considering and understanding the relationship as it evolves, and listening. Is the input from the other beneficial to my well-being or are things changing?

The guiding influences that we relate to in our lives need to have a foundation set in love.

The love should look like kindness, gentleness, patience, peace-seeking and forgiving. This will look like a well-meaning towards each other in regular contacts and, for me, is a serving each other as fellow human beings. The love that we see in society, especially noticeable in the pandemic, is an expression of the Spirit of Jesus living within us as the Holy Spirit.

Summary

As we proceed along our pathway, we are naturally stepping out and stepping forward. We are necessarily entering new environments, meeting new people and experiencing new drugs (substance or activity). As a result, we can feel anxious, and experience doubt.

We step back into a reliance on our instincts and seek advice from our guides. Our daily living encompasses a balancing act between risk and reward; at times conforming, other times taking a stride.

In essence we need to be mindful that we can be drawn into a response that is not of our self. Because that choice fits in with what appears to be socially acceptable, it may not be acceptable to ourselves. The environment we inhabit can have a detrimental influence on our choices (in this case imprisonment). We can benefit from pulling over and seeking a neutral standpoint and an empathic view – a friend, an ally.

Questions

- Do you seek space away from environments, in order to reflect on the relationships you have?
- How important is listening to you, do you find it easy or difficult; why?
- Would it be helpful to introduce regime to your day-to-day life; why?
- How does freedom look to you?

Journal

Chapter Five

Friend at the Bar

If "two's company, three's a crowd", but how about four or more? What if the third is cocaine, for example; what if the fourth is 4,000 people?

How a relationship changes, positively or negatively, when the traffic becomes congested needs to be taken into account for each of us. The reference to 4,000 is obviously an indication of the company generated by social media. This environment will be covered in the next chapter, as it is huge and relevant to many lives.

Take a look at two dramas, delivered in workshops, that explore how different personalities alter when in conversation. Some impose, some agree with everything, some listen and make thoughtful comments.

Shared experience

Cannabis

Scene: bench in park, friends that regularly hang out.

Sophie – Did you know we can get cannabis here if we want to?

James – Yeah, my brother used to.

Sophie – Does he still smoke? I suppose it chills him out, being your brother.

James – Ha-ha. As it happens, he has been acting a bit strange, a bit tetchy, especially towards my parents. I am not sure he can afford to use as much as he wants; he's not in work.

Sophie – We should all have freedom of choice. We have got all the information through the Net, and don't forget, many people use it as a medicine against pain and mental-health problems.

Rachel – You know that do you? We are all different and just because someone says it on social media and they have hundreds of likes doesn't mean it represents all of us!

Sophie – Wow! You woke up on the wrong side of the bed this morning, calm down. I think you need a puff. I can make my own decisions, thank you.

Cannabis – I hear this debate all the time. What they don't understand is that I have many sides; in my natural state Sophie is right I can be a healer. However, since man started on the greed thing, I'm the dealer!

James – Rachel, are you OK? I mean we are all friends aren't we, Sophie?

Rachel – Guys, I bought some last night here in the park. Not sure how I feel today, but last night I felt kind of relaxed, but also had a feeling of not being in control. Not sure I could have smoked more.

James – Don't forget it's illegal. The way Sophie talks, you would think we were living in a legalised state.

Sophie – Let's all just chill out.

Cannabis – It's interesting in this country at the moment. The Internet makes everyone an expert, people follow trends without even thinking it through most of the time. At the end of the day, tens of thousands of people enjoy a joint – we all need to chill out don't we? Can you afford it?

New psychoactive drugs (previously "legal highs")

Scene: high street, friends witnessing a man acting weirdly.

Troy – Look at that guy, is he a street-entertainer trying to balance on the edge of the fountain?

Maisie – Kind of funny. But not sure he's totally in control, he's acting weird.

Luke – Got to film this. Whoops, he's gone and fallen in!

Troy – Now, that is entertaining, he's got to be on something; he doesn't seem to care. (Shouts) Go on mate!

Maisie – Don't just stand there, go and help him out you two!

Luke – Just spoken to someone; they said "Beware the Cookie monster!"

Maisie – Is that his nickname?

Troy – No, it's what he's taken, a legal high; that guy was having great fun.

Luke – You're behind the times, they are illegal to produce, supply and take. The Cookie monster imitates a cannabinoid substance; can freak you out obviously!

Maisie – Sounds cool! I like cookies.

Luke – You're fifteen not five, Maisie. He is liable to do anything under the influence.

Troy – Don't think it's funny for him any more, he's under the water!

Maisie – I really think you should help him, boys. NOW!

Later ...

Luke – He's OK, just spoken to his mate. He saw the brand name online, saw a funny YouTube clip, bought some and ended up in A & E.

Maisie – Bit like what we thought when we saw him – encouraged him, filmed it and would probably have posted it.

Luke – Yeah, I have.

Maisie – Bloody idiot!

Troy – Seemed like he was having fun – the way it affected him.

Luke/Maisie – DON'T EVEN GO THERE!

It is inevitable that when we move along our pathway, that is daily life, that environments that we enter and interact with influence us. We recall that, internally, we are guided by an instinct born out of experiences from relationships. How we react is dependent on many factors – variables. Our self has boundaries that, if pushed, affect our mood and actions. However, we have choice and, hopefully, we pause, think and assess our involvement. This is the reset.

The dramas present interaction for different people with substances that are currently illegal. We, as individuals and as a collective (that is society's view), will entertain relationships for different reasons. We bring differing perspectives to a group situation. We recall that each of us is shaped differently through our environments. Some present as leaders, some as followers, some as rebels, some conformists, if you like. In addition, we could present a drama on legal and prescribed substances such as diazepam, codeine or temazepam. The interaction with these, within a relationship that originates on medical grounds, can alter with use, bringing about similar reactions, thoughts and outcomes.

Many people can experience a range of thoughts and feelings that can impact positively and negatively through activities. We could replace friend at the bar with friend down the gym, or friend down the betting shop/or online game.

When we look at how we spend our time, twenty-four hours a day and seven days a week, we see time spent in company (relationship). In addition, some time is spent in self-contemplation, reflecting on how we are today. Do I consider those conversations or that activity useful? Have I received the enjoyment, learnt something or been reassured by that interaction?

There are factors that influence how we feel and impact on our general well-being. We may ask ourselves some questions when in a time of reflection or review. Do I feel under pressure to join in with this? When I am there is it me that is there, or is it a person that is expected to be there, but not revealing myself and my views? Does it matter? Does my outside represent my inside? It might not matter, but it may if and when the relationship(s) goes deeper.

These may seem like long drawn-out self-examinations that don't matter; provided I am content, safe and joining in, or belonging to, then it's OK. However, they may become more relevant to physical and mental health, if the relationship with the activity, substance, person/people changes.

So what are we like in traffic? Do we shout, shout the loudest and we will be the one heard, joining in with everyone else sounding their horn? Are we patient and understanding, thinking that I will see the way ahead eventually?

There are pressure-point situations of which we need to be aware. The socially acceptable phrase, that we spoke of earlier, can bring on a certain amount of pressure in itself.

I recall a conversation that I had in prison.

Shared experience

I was speaking with someone who had found themselves in prison as a result of assaulting someone while under the influence of alcohol. He generally enjoyed a drink, as most do that choose to drink. However, on this occasion, he met a group of mates that were drinking a lot; more than he would normally. He joined in, and, when he drank too much he could get aggressive. He took something the wrong way, hit someone and caused injury (he had previous). He was taken to the police station, remanded in prison as all police cells were full. He told me how things had occurred.

"We all drink don't we, Guv [inmates would call us this]? It's socially acceptable."

> I said, "So what you are saying is that we have to wait for society to change [in terms of its view on alcohol and in particular drinking too much], in order for you to stop coming into prison? I don't see any of your friends in here with you."
>
> We spoke about risk and reward, his relationship with alcohol and what he has to gain or lose – a reset.

We see and hear this attitude every day; this is not exclusive to prison. The people I spoke to in prison were unable to manage their interactions with drugs and people, and would lose control. The consequences would often cause harm to them or others.

The vast majority of inmates I spoke to stated that alcohol had a bearing on their actions leading to imprisonment. It is easy to see how this can happen. A social situation where the drug is accepted by most of those present as part of the group, can be problematic to some. On most occasions, alcohol is an important participant who contributes much. The company may share this view with regard to cannabis, new psychoactive drugs, prescribed medications, cocaine, ecstasy and others. Each environment may contain company that has, collectively, socially accepted use.

What does society mean, with regard to our relationships? This is important, each of us makes up a community of people who socialise in groups – a society. Some are more socially aware than others. Others will choose to buck the trend, possibly coming across as anti-social. This does not necessarily mean creating trouble, but advancing a different view. This view/opinion, to the group, may create a rift or a disturbance.

It is useful to look at examples that are common today. The company within a bar, a party, a meeting to discuss an agenda; these are common social settings. We need to be aware of how pressure can be felt within certain situations, groups, and where there may be a drug present.

When we look at how our time is spent each day many may not even be aware of the time spent on social media, but it's not just the time. When we consider traffic, this relationship is undoubtedly, for many, the largest and most important on their pathway. We look at this next.

Summary

Many of the relationships we develop alter, over time, as others enter into the environment and the situation changes. Be they person or drug, substance or activity, individual or many; we may experience the interaction differently as it goes on.

Who we are with will affect our input and the response we give and, consequently, what we receive from the relationship. Choice is important, and our choice is based on our self and what our instinct is telling us.

Mood can change when the dynamics of the relationship are altered. Many drugs are seen as socially acceptable; many do not question their using as, if society says yes, who am I to say no. A list may include alcohol, cannabis, a number of prescribed anti-depressants/painkillers, legal highs (as was), types of gambling; there may be others that you might consider. The risk and damage can be to the individual where an imbalance occurs and the relationship becomes unsafe.

Questions

- To what extent does the influence of what society says affect your views? Consider some of the environments that you inhabit.
- Which of the relationships that you engage in are socially acceptable; does that have a bearing on your use?
- What are you like in traffic?

Journal

Chapter Six

Resident or Visitor?

The relationship we have with social media is of a different construct than others spoken about so far. For a start the interaction ranges from occasional to permanent in terms of time spent in this relationship.

When we talk about the pathways that we each walk down, the relationship appears like the scenery you are walking through. In so far as it is ever-present (even if you don't interact that often); it is easy to be distracted by it and you can stop and look at, interact with it.

A house with many rooms

When we discuss it in workshops, we sometimes use the analogy of approaching a house with a door that is closed. It may not be a house you recognise and, with the door closed, you are unsure who lives there. Therefore, when you open the door you cannot be sure of who might be there, how many live there, how many different rooms there may be and who lives in them. What might the rooms contain? It may be a house you recognise. The person who opens the door is recognisable to you. There may be different and/or more guests in the rooms. In this analogy, the rooms might represent topics/subjects of interest being discussed or debated; which room feels comfortable, safe, and which contains a feeling of trepidation?

Social media, through all the devices used, facilitates relationships. Today we are residents or visitors, as regards our relationship with social media. Residents inhabit a natural state of being on using social media, and thus do not select when to use. Visitors log on to it, and interact, then at a later point log off. We mention a natural state because many have now been brought up on it and daily life, for the most part, revolves around it. It is a primary care-giver.

We are not saying that either state is wholly healthy or unhealthy to the well-being of any one person. Indeed, our relationship (however we were to describe it) with social media, via any device, is with person/people and it is a drug. The relationship is subject to changes in intensity, incurs problems, pleases, teaches, exposes vulnerability, threatens boundaries, develops identity and is subject to the variables that exist within us and around us.

It might be useful to look at a drama involving a group and, of course, a phone – the social-media enabler.

Shared experience

Social media

Scene: friends meeting up with the phone being part of the group.

Phone – You need me.

Joe – No way; I pick and choose.

Cara – You've never chosen to not answer it, let alone switch it off.

Joe – I've got friends, got to stay in touch.

Gary – Hi, Joe, let's go to Abi's party.

Joe – Let me notify everyone.

Gary – What if EVERYONE doesn't want to come?

Phone – Sense a bit of anxiety here, if I don't light up in the next few minutes.

Cara – Hey you two, chill out, talk it over.

Joe – Hey Gary, don't really feel like going around Abi's.

Gary – Yeah, sure, I guess Abi ISN'T ON SOCIAL MEDIA ENOUGH.

Phone – You know what? People used to use me – now I use them.

Cara – I said talk it over; you have known each other for years. By the way, I hope you're both going to get behind that social-media campaign about increasing the cost of an alcohol unit – post a comment!

Joe – I'm not sure.

Gary – WHAT? Don't you know, everyone's done it – IT'S GONE VIRAL.

Phone – And you thought I offer everybody an opportunity to voice their opinion – not always.

Joe – Cara?

Cara – Yes, Joe.

> **Joe** – Me and Gary know you use your phone just as much as us. Be careful, we are your friends, but there are a lot of weirdos out there.
>
> **Cara** – What do you mean? I'm entitled to my opinion; I happen to feel strongly about the effects of alcohol.
>
> **Gary** – That's not what Joe means Cara; we were shown some pictures, just be careful OK?
>
> **Cara** – Oh … OK, thanks.
>
> Phone – They have a choice: be selective to your own needs and wants – let me be part, not all of your life.

It is useful to include the phone as part of the conversation, as we have already seen how the other is an active participant. The other has personality, especially so in the case of social media. However, in this case, social media can present with a face, without a face or with multiple faces. In this respect the user can be presented with interaction that can present difficulty. In addition we can see from the drama that people respond differently and that can have a knock-on effect to other relationships.

You may read the conversation and see yourself in a particular role. When discussing this scenario, we may advance the argument or opinion of Joe, Cara or Gary. What are your feelings about the observations made by the phone? This drug really has a voice, and definitely speaks in conversations through links to adverts/articles that it knows might maintain your interest.

There is a camaraderie between them, and yet, bring interactions with social media into the situation and there is change. All three engage with others on the phone, from what we read they have different relationships. This is no surprise as they are three separate people who use social media. Now they will agree on some reasons that they use social media, but some may differ.

Our engagement

What does your phone represent to you? If resident, you might say that you need to talk to people and that's how we do it (rather than arrange to meet). Even so, many with phones also experience a whole range of feelings when interacting. With this relationship on the one hand there is no question that it is socially acceptable. However, engagement on a personal level can engender different feelings. The fact that it is such a universal part of daily life brings certain concerns to an individual. How will my view be appraised; I know that even if I sent it to one person, it can be shared with any other number? There can be an anxiety connected to a vulnerability. In addition, how will a response be seen, acceptable or to be castigated?

These examples can be seen regularly in the flow of traffic, that is social media. The relationship ebbs and flows rapidly; this is inevitable when so many people are at the table sharing. The issue for most is that not to be at the table is a non-starter. We must not forget that we have two generations that have been brought up with this relationship being one of a care-giver. However, it is really important that we seek our individual needs; what is my relationship with this other? Is it a companion, an opportunity to use for gain, and to make my voice heard? These appear to be valuable aspects to the self and life-changing. Sometimes though, the fact that we are using an intermediary that leaves a footprint (image, or something said) may bring about indecision, anxiety, even a perceived threat to your self.

It can be useful to look at an alternative drama that centres on gaming (a drug), and includes a device and its interaction with users.

Shared experience

Gaming

Scene: mum and sons, and another, along with the device.

Console – I'm part of the group – the device.

Gary – Where have you been?

Joe – Mum wanted to ask me about the game we bought. I said it's just a game and everyone's playing it!

Gary – What does she want to know for? I know people playing it and they're not starting to shoot people on the streets!

Console – I think Mum's heard there's another side to gaming, but she's not sure what. She's right, but I'm their mate; I will look after them.

Joe – Gary?

Gary – What?

Joe – Let's join that server, there's a guy that's been messaging me. Might take us on to the next level; I NEED ANOTHER CHALLENGE, you're miles behind.

Gary – I've been letting you get ahead, I know how you sulk. Who is it? We don't know them.

Joe – That's why we talk; there's no reason why we can't play with him or her. Hi, I'm Joe, I'm six . . . teen.

Console – The boys are enjoying themselves, that's good. Who's the guy? Hello, Mum's at the door.

Mum – Hi, boys, who's winning? I think I would be good at this.

Gary – Mum, there is an age restriction!

Joe – We are fine, this guy just joined us.

Mum – Who is he? Where is he?

Gary – He isn't here; he likes games, just like us, but is not with us.

Mum – Well, if you're enjoying yourselves, have a good time. Call it a day in an hour.

The guy – You are joking, your mum was going to play– how old are you?

Gary – Like Joe said, we are sixteen, we are twins.

The guy – We both like the same things, we'll have to talk more. But seriously, not your mum!

Console – Hang on boys, you look young for sixteen, aren't you thirteen? I thought we were just playing a game. Now we are meeting others – who is he?

Gary – Let's play

Later . . .

Gary – Hey mate, what is your name anyway; we have to go soon?

The guy – No problem, guys; if you look online you will see a request for password, personal details, user name, etc. What do you like to do Joe, when you're not gaming? I bet you're interested in all sorts of things.

Joe – Yeah, course.

The guy – Maybe we could meet up; what do you like doing?

Gary – Let's go Joe, good to meet you, mate.

Console – Gaming's fine, but in a relationship you need to know the other person and be yourself. By the way, the guy is mum's new boyfriend, why is he asking these questions?

In this scenario you can see a number of variables coming into play. Once more we can see the participants within the relationship coming from different places; each seeing the interaction from a different view. Mum wants to engage with her boys and the other, the gaming, but the relationship is not what she expects. Her agenda is encouraging, but watchful because she doesn't know enough. The boys want to enjoy gaming; at the same time they are having to give more (reveal), than they anticipated. We have already spoken about stepping forward and with it, a pressure to follow, to belong – because "everybody's doing it, aren't they?". This will be a recurrent theme within this genre of relationship. We know who the guy is (they don't), and we think we know his agenda, but no face. The drug is just available and constant, it is the interactions with it that are variable and unpredictable at times. We need to remind ourselves that the fact that gaming is referred to as a drug, which it is (see Glossary), the outcome of any relationships can be beneficial and/or of a harmful nature.

We need to explore, in more depth, the type of relationship that social media presents whether you are resident or visitor. The communication enabled is person-to-person, or people, and the structure allows for different modes of communication. We can call and talk, but many choose to message through text and images, fixed or videoed. This flexibility provides each user with an opportunity to remain in relationship and, at the same time, measure their involvement or commitment.

As discussed, we are all coming from different places dependent on how we feel, the mood that we are in and with respect to our self. At any moment, our instinct may tell us: be bold, be careful, don't even go there, comment but keep it to yourself, or give it both barrels! Social media offers us a screen; not just in a physical sense but as a barrier to stand behind.

Shared experience

When I spoke to young people about their relationship with social media, we spoke about text or talk. The opinion, generally, was that they would not always be comfortable with speaking and then having to respond immediately, or speaking and sounding like this or that, maybe giving a certain impression (or sensing the same in a reply). So messaging was a safer option, although even how that is interpreted can sometimes compromise us.

The image we present

Within a society, where, how we present ourselves, matters so much to so many. The content of social media and how it is presented are important. Why? We come back to the essence of why we are relational beings. We seek others, the person and the drug, to develop our identity – our image. We seek to belong, our instincts are born out of a herd mentality – to follow; we are tribal with leaders and followers.

We are all influenced by society and what it says, to a lesser or greater extent, some of it age-related. Many that are resident, where their natural state is to maintain a constant dialogue with society, will respond and react to that dialogue. How the messages are received has an impact on our engagement. The communication will be presented with the personality and the character of the other; an image will be portrayed and we will respond according to the variables we have covered. Before responding, in many cases, it would be useful to pause, reflect and consider how we feel about what we are hearing, seeing, or being told. However, with many communications there is a pressure to respond quickly; to agree and show that agreement.

How often have we felt that to pause and consider our next interaction might be seen as disagreement, a negative comment, and even opposition? The relationship with social media and its facilitation of connection with one, few or many can be a fast ride and difficult to get off. We have to consider the vulnerability of some of us; the young, those with mental-health concerns, experiencing low points, the elderly, those that just don't seem to fit.

Dealing with the traffic

Relationships within the genre of social media can introduce static* into a life. Static can lead to mixed messages and confusion where someone might be looking for clarity within a conversation. Earlier we spoke about simplification, in terms of the environments we interact with and the company therein. The pathway can become congested and the traffic difficult to navigate. There is no question that the enhanced ability to engage with many through multiple platforms is a good fit with our relational selves. The benefits to the individual, within this relationship, include more opportunities for personal growth, broadening the mind, forming opinion and boosting confidence.

Our involvement is a choice; however, the part of ourselves that requires to belong, to conform and participate because of a societal pressure, can easily turn the visitor into the resident. Whether that is healthy and fruitful can depend on how each of us listens to our self. How does this fit with my boundaries of safety, security, what does the risk-to-reward ratio look like, and how does this relationship affect the reality of my day-to-day life? The resident may need to step out and make connection again with the surface off the road that they are walking on.

Shared experience

How we present to others in any medium is important to how we are received. I try to reach out with kindness and support – through love, with the Holy Spirit guiding.

Summary

The relationship that is social media allows for platforms of communication at anytime, anywhere. It is a natural state for many people to utilise this facility to inform themselves of what is being said in society. From how everyone in the family, and how friends are, to trends developing in society and what I might support and what I might oppose.

Like all relationships, the other has a personality and contributes, and this continues backwards and forwards. However, this conversation can be multiplied many times over; in this respect, each individual will experience an array of feelings and emotions because we are different.

The fit with us as human beings is very attractive and the rewards can enhance us in terms of confidence and reputation. At the same time, our participation in the conversations can expose us to harm and it can prove very difficult to step away, to deny ourselves through the addictiveness of involvement, and the cost of withdrawal.

Questions

- When you consider people that you engage with on social media, who do you see as resident/visitor, and how do you see yourself?
- How do you see the relationship; do you feel controlled in relation to what you say?
- What would your friends say about the relationship, same as you or different?

Journal

Chapter Seven
Role Model

If our primary care-givers are not role models, what happens next?

We envisage a role model as one who portrays a life, day-to-day, that is good practice to copy. They will demonstrate traits of character that are generally admired. You may see confidence, a positive attitude, genuine, respectful and generous in word and deed.

We have already spoken about how we present ourselves to others within the environments we live – our relationships. Our outlook is shaped by the interactions we experience, our own instincts, and the many variables at play. Our choice of company is determined by our needs or our wants; a sense of belonging and to be loved, a desire to learn and develop as human beings. It is the way we respond and the way we act towards the other, that shapes who we are.

Those that may be described as role models have also been shaped through the same process. Previously we have considered how our type (the character that we are) tends to be leader or follower, in how we react in situations with others. In essence we are all individuals, walk our own pathways and encounter traffic and react to it in different ways. What part does a role model play in this?

We have to approach the establishment of role models, within our relationship framework, with care.

Shared experience

When working in the prison you could easily step into the role of the care-giver, in as much as taking action on behalf of the client (inmate). You could portray a way of walking forward on a particular pathway that you thought they should take. It is right, for example, that certain arrangements needed to be put in place when someone is going out into the community. However, the individual has to take the steps and plan their way forward. The person will be re-entering an environment that they lived in, in terms of company, and will have to make choices on relationships: those to continue, those to end, and those that they may wish to engage. They have to live their life.

We have to be aware that in our normal daily life there is a balance to be found. Who or what (person or drug) may give me company that is safe, that I will benefit from and that I will feel happy and positive about?

What does our role model look like?

So how does the role model fit? Initially, we should be careful to not base our view on first impressions. We have looked at how the inside, the self that we are, does not always represent the outside – what people see. Through all the various relationships we have explored, there can be a big difference between how we experience one another. This change can happen in an instance dependent on the variables at play. We have mentioned the word "portray" a couple of times in this chapter; a role can be like a part played by someone. It is important to be aware that a role model may be portraying themselves with certain characteristics that appear admirable; however, as a relationship develops, will they be sustained? They did not choose to be a role model for you; you did the choosing.

During a relationship, they may be completely unaware that they are being observed. There is a need to build a relationship with care and attention. We benefit from checking in with ourselves, our instincts and our feelings. We do need to step out, and the role model may be a positive step. You may take the view that, when new to an environment, a guide that knows the road is useful. However, it is the case that the other has their own agenda, what they themselves want from the interaction, and there will be a number of variables affecting their presentation.

If you re-examine the characters within the dramas previously presented, you may identify with one or two. If you placed yourself in the scenario, is this how you might have responded to the others? Alternatively, you may have seen what was said and how the character responded to others as a good role model in that situation.

Why we need a role model

Why would we consider a role model, as a concept that would benefit us as individuals? We have maybe had a bad experience with someone (or a drug) that has knocked us back. We may have entered a new environment; a workplace or an activity or a new home, where we are seeking a guide that appears used to that environment. It maybe that we are restarting our life with different primary care-givers who we need to provide a sound foundation.

These examples are junctions on our pathways. Would identifying a role model assist us in making our way forward safely and bringing the reassurance we are seeking? The role model is held up as someone who is known to be confident, a positive influence, maybe someone who is respected and generous with their time. However, it may not be what they are portraying to the outside world in their environment. It is what we_are seeking in terms of a relationship to enable us to step forward. The important factor in this, is that it is *you* that is stepping forward, in whatever direction at the junction, and not them.

Clearly, to have a source of advice from someone, that may be known as family or friends, and that others in the family can testify to, can be beneficial: but this is different from over-relying on an other that we have encountered within the environment. The journey being made is our journey, mistakes will be made along the way, but our pathway is a learning experience. In terms of the pathway that we are on; you will trip, who doesn't, but falling and hurting oneself is compounding the problem. We should treat the situation as we would any other possible relationship, by trusting our instincts, being mindful of our self as we meet others.

If we look at the example of the other guy in the drama around gaming, we can see how a young person can step out, without care, and risk exploitation from an older person with an agenda.

We can find that someone who presents to others as confident, maybe over-confident, and outspoken in an environment, may be accepted as a role model. This person will often be a leader in terms of personality type. Consequently, they may have a following; this scenario can quite often be played out on social media as well as on the street.

In fact, social media can add another layer of complication to someone who is looking for a way forward at a junction reached on their pathway. Without the ability to assess another through closeness, the real world; we can, through the portrayal of an image and/or an announced view, see another as a role model. The outcome can be positive and lead to encouragement, reassurance that someone shares my view; though we have to be aware that the anonymity this environment offers, can allow someone to portray a number of different roles.

Taking time to consider

We can only rely on our experiences along our pathway, how relationships that we have built have impacted on us, and listen to our primary and secondary care-givers. At any junction that we arrive at to listen first is preferable. To listen before we speak (take a step forward and commit) will, in the long term, benefit us: too many speak before they think and find that a relationship, in any medium, encounters difficulties. We need to gather our thoughts and consider our options; too many times we feel obliged (pressurised) to respond quickly.

So where is freedom for the individual in all this? How does the role model contribute to the development of the self? The freedom to express oneself with confidence and to be self-assured is a destination to be reached for on the pathway ahead. The role model, as a guide along the way, can be an asset especially for those who have experienced setbacks. A role model may have travelled the same road and "been there and done it". We always have to be aware that they may have their own agenda. For, after all, we have, in the way in which we have chosen to follow them. We also have to see the bigger picture. Take this as an example: we may meet them in a bar, be encouraged by the way they appear to us, and then, through suggestion, choose to drink excessively and take cocaine for the first time. We spoke about this scenario earlier with the conversation I had within the prison. This sequence of events is not unusual. We can see the process repeated in many other relationships involving substances both legal and illegal, and gambling scenarios as well.

> ## *Shared experience*
>
> *Gambling*
>
> **Scene:** high street.
>
> Dave, Simon and Winbig (a slot game with a £100 prize every 1,000 plays).
>
> **Dave** – Hi Simon, how you doing?
>
> **Simon** – Fine.
>
> **Dave** – You don't look it. Let's go and spend some money, sales are on!
>
> **Simon** – I haven't got any as usual. Unlike you, I haven't got a job.
>
> **Dave** – It's not just my wages. I had a win on Winbig.

> *Simon* – Is that the game you play on your phone?
>
> *Winbig* – Dave is a game player, and most of the time he forgets he is gambling; maybe a chance here to gain another player.
>
> *Dave* – Yeah, got a good pay-out, but still waiting for the big one, £100. It's all about the timing.
>
> *Simon* – I suppose the more players of Winbig, the quicker it will happen. Send me the link, I need some new stuff.
>
> *Winbig* – It's strange, they say they don't have any or much money, but always seem to find it. But they are game players, spending hours gaming, it's easy to switch. Just look at the balance sheet, I could easily afford to give away £1,000.
>
> *Simon* – Dave, how much do I bet?
>
> *Dave* – Bet? I don't really spend much at all, I get some free spins.
>
> *Winbig* – Well done Dave, I couldn't have said it better myself. It's a bit of fun!

This scenario is played out repeatedly within a number of environments. The players are coming from different places; one person is interacting with a situation that is new to them. The other person may be observed as the role model; here, there is an existing relationship as mates, then another is introduced. The first person is looking for guidance. The second guy assumes this role, being a friend, but also building themselves up as one to be trusted.

As we are aware from earlier dramas, the third "person" also plays an active role. The scenario then plays out. The outcome, in terms of the relationship and the risks and rewards, will follow: however, we can see how the role-model relationship has to be approached with eyes open. The expression of oneself, within any relationship, within any environment by listening to your self is desirable.

The role model as an interaction is helpful where one is being taught a specific task. For example, when going to a gym, for the first time, to embark on improving fitness and feeling better for it. A professional is advisable to demonstrate the way forward for you. It is a new environment, your health and safety need to be safeguarded; otherwise, with poor advice, we may be led down a different path.

In terms of primary care-givers; parents/carers and other family, as well as teachers to the young, should be role models to their "cared-for". With regard to the development of the young individual into a confident, self-assured adult; a strong foundation based on trust and with their best interests at heart is an advantage. The introduction of the role model as a relationship to be sought to guide along the pathway, needs to be considered in just the same way as any other interaction.

Summary

The existence of role models within society is generally seen as a benefit. When seeking relationships, a role model within the company we keep can offer learning and guidance that can be trusted. However, we need to be mindful that some relationships that offer this support can mislead. They can be portraying themselves outwardly in order to present a front that doesn't always represent their true purpose. As in all interaction within the environments you inhabit, we need to listen and consider before we step forward.

There are certain benefits to seeking a role model in so far as, where specific tasks need to be demonstrated to safeguard our interests. Thus the teacher, when young, and professional adviser when older; and, the primary care-giver providing a secure and sound foundation that can be trusted.

Questions

- Who are the role models in your life?
- Do you feel that you play that part for others in any environment?
- As you participate on social media, are you influenced by the presence of people; how?

Journal

Chapter Eight

Relationships: The Family Space

We should return to the origin of relationship; the parents and child(ren), to understand more of our relational selves. What should the environment look like in order to cultivate an understanding of which relationships to seek, and the reasons to do so? We want the child to step out and interact, to give and receive and develop themselves whilst safeguarding. We hope that the family environment, the home and the people, are bound together by common cause. The primary care-giver and the cared-for, being the parent and the child, interacting within a maternal/paternal love. However, this is not always the case due to changes in circumstance that call for adaptability, whereby there can be role-reversal. Nevertheless, the roles, with their differences, should exist in order to facilitate growth for both the younger and the older.

Parent and child – the interaction

The parent engages as an adult who has experienced life as a young person into an adult with responsibilities: and the child receiving from the parent to grow and develop their own senses.

The environment will be shaped in terms of how everyone experiences each other; parent-to-parent, parent-to-child and child-to-parent. How that, in turn, makes them feel, affects the way they portray themselves. We do not always play out the role of parent and of child in the way we interact; the impact of external factors may change the attitudes of either. Therefore, the environment or space can look and feel different within the home, by each that lives there.

So how might the space look and feel? Importantly the space should be a place of acceptance that can benefit all parties. Each person, within the family space, will have an identity that they wish to explore, develop and protect. Each will also, knowing their role (parent/child), need to not only feel that they are accepted in that role; but also as a developing individual, a personality of their own. This is the same for all of us regardless of age and relationship to others within the home. Acceptance is an important element within the space. It allows for growth when it is part of the relationships within the home. It encompasses a listening aspect and a respect that can make all parties feel better. The important consideration is that it is a two-way thing. The space needs to represent a place where communication is encouraged and thoughts shared. In addition, an acknowledgement of each, the child and the parent, of the responsibilities that they have within the environment.

Shared experience

When in conversation with a group of young people, we were talking about important relationships.

I was asked about my relationship with my mother. I said that it was a friendship, but also with a respect for her as my mother. Sometimes she spoke to me reminding me to do this or that, like she had always done. Other times we spoke as two adults about a piece of news or gossip.

One of the young people (teenagers) said that her mother was her best friend. We spoke about what they meant in day-to-day situations; the difference between a child-to-parent and a child-to-friend relationship.

This scenario illustrates how we adopt different roles within the family environment. The allowance of a space where communication is invited and there is a listening, can make sharing easier.

A good example would be the use of social media within the home. As we have previously covered, this is a relationship that many of all ages engage in. Therefore, there is common ground between everyone at home. There is also an acceptance that it will be interacted with in a number of different ways. The parental perspective may include the safeguarding of the child, dependent on the age of the child of course. The perspective of the child may vary from "this is my space", to sharing with others in the home (as well as interaction with friends). When the space in the home environment is an accepting one, that encourages open communication and respect; sharing of information being normal. From a safeguarding point of view, involvement in one another's relationship with social media is beneficial to both the parent and the child. Therefore, an enquiry by either into what the other is engaged with on social media, will be seen as an interest and not an intrusion.

Shared experienced

Child – I have just started using this app, Mum.

Parent – Let's have a look; is it something that I could use too?

Child – Yeah, why not?

Parent – Thanks. I have started using this sounds app – interesting stories.

Child – I'll take a look.

This exchange may or may not happen (in this way), but demonstrates how the space is healthy and acknowledges both parties. The child feels comfortable sharing, the parent takes an interest and encourages joint-use. The child accepts, and because they do the parent makes the same offer.

A healthy space

In the same way, other areas of possible challenge such as sexuality, mood changes, changes in family structure, etc. can become more manageable. The relationship within the home is also enhanced by a space where we speak, but also listen. We have looked at the mechanics of relationship, examining output and input; and how the tone and content impact on the self. The space within the home environment will remain healthy where there is an interest in hearing the other. In fact, to listen first, before responding. When this doesn't happen, we incur traffic (too many voices clashing), leading to mixed messages. When we have a situation where many are speaking, and listening doesn't happen, the parent and child can adopt different positions. So, the parent can look and sound different to the child, and similarly, the child will respond in a different way.

The relationship will incur changes like this due to a number of factors. The young person is altering, through growth and development, and the dynamics of the engagement with the parent change. Where there is a space that encourages acceptance, a listening and love; these changes can be accommodated.

The binding element within the environment of the relationship is love. The parent and child interaction should exist within a framework of love for one another. That framework consisting of a kindness and gentleness alongside an understanding and forgiving nature.

There is growth, from a baby, to young child, into teenage years and older. The parent may be seen as a "best friend" as mentioned, but they are still the mother/father. The child becoming the young person will, of course, change in character as they interact with other secondary relationships. At times, comparisons will be made between the internal relationships in other family environments with their own.

The young person, through the increased confidence of gained experiences, may challenge previously accepted communication within the space. The dynamic between parent and child changes position. When these situations arise the family space, if it has retained a sense of acceptance within a framework of love, will adapt.

Interaction outside the family space

At the same time the parent will have also experienced changes in their daily lives. Their role will have evolved as the age of the child increases. The parent, having been a child of course, will know of the external forces that the child is exposed to. They will also encounter different relationships and, at times, look at themselves as parents compared to other parents. This may not always be healthy, as you will not be privy to the home space of the other.

This is why it is important to have the anchor points, within their own space; those identifiable and instinctive roles of parent and child. Through external relationships each experiences; the way that we feel about each other and ourselves alters. Our mood swings one way and another, and this has an impact on the primary care-giver to the cared-for relationship. Different points of views and attitudes will be brought into the space; as a result the space will need to keep allowing the sharing and listening. This is why the space is important, it grants both the parent and the child a place where they can comment.

Cultivating the space

Where this space is cultivated by the family and valued as a place of safety from early on; growth and development by all is accommodated. Another area where the space created is of advantage, is within the step-parent situation: as it is an open space where exchange of views can take place that offers all parties a voice. Once again it is important to maintain the integrity which includes an opportunity for listening and sharing within a safe environment. It may be the case that the different families and the relationships within them, engage in different ways. For example, the parent-to-child relationship in one is strained, there is little communication with space closed off. The other may sustain an environment which encourages discussion and acceptance of other opinion. There will be a chance that exposure to a space like this will affect change.

The nurturing of a space which is acceptable to all family members from early on can assist in smoothing over the rough patches that all families have to contend with. This approach can clearly bring out a sense of a "friend" aspect at times which reflects a comfort with each other. Furthermore, there is no reason why a space dimension to the family environment can't be grown where there is a will to make things work.

When we look at the family space a certain freedom of speech may exist. This should always be regulated by a consideration, by the parent and the child, of their place within the family space. Although an openness is encouraged and benefits all, there will always be a need for fixed anchor points. These points, which look to safeguard parent and child, ensure that the freedom remains comfortable for all.

We were not born with a role. We are relational beings that form our own characters through our experiences within relationships, shaping our environments. Yes, we are a child that may become a parent and therefore adopt a position in relation to others; but this is not all we are. However, the familiarity and the safeguarding of the family space offers a stability when, as individuals, we experience the variety of moods from exposure to other environments.

Summary

The parent and child relationship is one that is bound by a love that unites. In order to establish interaction that enables growth for all, a recognised space can be agreed. This family space allows individual expression and acceptance which can assist in overcoming challenges. There can be a security found that reinforces both parent and child as the relationship evolves.

Questions

- Is there an understanding within your family space?
- Do you, as a child or a parent, feel comfortable to express yourself and the way that you feel as an individual?

Journal

Chapter Nine

Relationships: The Mental-Health Perspective

Throughout all the previous chapters we have observed and commented on the state of mental health. The freedom and the imprisonment we feel, at any given time, declares our state of being. We all experience a constant movement along a spectrum that declares to the outside world: "I feel comfortable in this situation and can relate to what is happening around me positively", to "I feel uncomfortable, unsafe and disassociated from the situation I am in"; and to many points in between.

As we live in a world where we experience relationships in all the forms we have covered; the way we feel, changes. It does so because the environment does not stand still. We move and are moved by circumstances around us. The interactions we have in any form, impact on our self and alter our feelings to varying degrees.

How these feelings realise themselves, differs in each and every individual. Within the dramas, we have observed and commented on the different reactions to what has been shared in the group. There have been strong opinions voiced, shared views and a listening and calming voice from others.

There are a multitude of reasons, from past experiences to communication difficulties for an individual, that can influence how someone receives and processes incoming messages. We need to be mindful of the communication channels we use and the environments we choose to participate in, in order to maintain a stability of self.

Is my own space a good (safe) place to be in? Can I rely on people around me, that know me and that I can call my care-givers, either primary or secondary? How do I feel about the company that I keep?

Identifying and adapting to change

In order to safeguard ourselves, we need to review the company and situations as things change. We, and the people that we are in contact with, all experience movement along a mental-health spectrum. At any given time, a mood swing can occur in response to something that has happened and affected someone we know. Someone may have heard bad news that is preying on their mind. Their mood will be affected, but it won't necessarily be revealed but it might be sensed by others. We need to look after each other's mental health, be aware that we are living out our lives in different areas. It is a fluid situation and this is where the listening is important.

The impact of the Covid-19 pandemic

In terms of things that change, the pandemic brought about a change in situation for all of us. The mental-health spectrum that we had been travelling both backwards and forwards on experienced a severe jolt.

In fairly quick time we were all exposed to relationship with Covid-19. Of course, our association with it differed from individual to individual. Many were infected, others not, but they were aware of the possibility. There were degrees of effect on individuals from the virus and, tragically, much loss of life alongside long periods of care required and recuperation. In addition, infection that did not lead to severe consequences to health physically but led to much distress psychologically. Naturally, people known to sufferers, be they friend, family or care providers, felt this.

The pandemic entered people's environments uninvited and altered our state of being. All of the relationships that we are in contact with at home, work, leisure, in various places that we had formed an opinion of, took on another meaning. Our instinct, as we have discussed, creates an understanding of the other, in terms of safety, benefit, risk and opportunity for growth.

Who is this stranger? I have a new relationship in my life that I am ignorant of through the self that I rely on. The only things that I will know about this stranger will be known through third parties – government, health service and social media. This scenario can be unnerving with regard to mental health. The relationships that we form have a structure to them that meets certain criteria, as we have already seen. We have seen how the pandemic has impacted upon others, some of whom we may know. This is not just the effect of infection but also how they feel.

Each of us will seek more information about the pandemic (the stranger in our environment). What do we know about it? What does it mean for me and people around me? Importantly, if I don't know as much as I feel I should, how should I react? In terms of our mental-health spectrum there will be a huge variation of positive and negative feelings.

The way in which each of us reacts will be determined by our individual assessment of risk. We will consider our past experiences of difficulties encountered in our lives; can we draw comparisons, how have I dealt with other circumstances? Who, within my circle of relationships both family and friends, will offer me a perspective that helps? Which of the environments I inhabit will offer more safety and reassurance? Whose company can I trust to learn more; the government, social media, my inner circle?

Our response to the unknown will be informed through a process of thought that is instinctive and designed to stabilise. In itself, it will explore the relational world we have formed around us, those relationships we have chosen, those that have always been there and others that are more fluid. There may be areas that we interact with much of the time, such as social media and various contacts. We have to be careful when listening to opinion as there are multiple sources that, in themselves, are strangers.

The pandemic has brought about another aspect of relationship. We have seen the engagement of people within communities. Within the community people have seen each other in the same struggle against a common adversary. As such we have seen the strength of teamwork, working together for the common good. This environment may have existed but not been seen as fertile ground for relationship. The exchange of goodwill and support for people struggling has benefited many from the young to the elderly and vulnerable. That benefit has boosted feelings of self-worth and of seeing each other in a new light. With regard to mental health, this reaction to the virus has had a positive effect.

Being good to ourselves – how to look after our own mental health

Is what I receive from others compatible with what I want or need? By listening to *ourselves* and others that we know and trust, we learn which situations are comfortable for us to be in. Some interactions can bring feelings of discomfort even threat. This is particularly relevant when we encounter new situations and therefore new people. There can be a risk that, if we are feeling fragile and in a depressed state, the relationship may increase our anxiety.

It is useful to consider what we are seeking from a relationship. Which qualities may a new relationship bring, and how do we instinctively feel.

Our instinct will sense when we are enjoying a positive experience; this sense is born out of past situations.

Exercise

Start off listing qualities that you look for in a relationship; you might include love, care, knowledge, enjoyment, peace, encouragement, sharing opinion, reassurance, empowerment, direction. You will find yourself reflecting on past experiences. Then make a list of environments that you move in, e.g. work, gym. Break this down to people that you know and speak to (maybe consider friends), how do they all match up? Any role models in there, any people that, when you look at them, actually don't match up? Any environments that are not proving to be a good fit for you today?

In terms of your mental health another key question is: "Am I strong enough to be myself with others, if not, why not?"

This is an internal dialogue that helps you to define where you struggle with your mental health. It also reveals where you may need to invest your time and energy. What is the proportion of people/drugs that give care to me within the places I interact with others that don't appear to invest in our relationship? We all need the assistance of care-givers in our lives in order to safeguard our mental health and well-being.

You might come up with the conclusion that a relationship, even an environment is not healthy. It follows that you have to take action; as the other may be continuing on without the same feeling. What do you have to look at?

How much time and energy do you use in maintaining a relationship? Can I use my time more productively in another area? It might surprise you to calculate time devoted to someone or something, and how you may be giving up something or someone else. If you have a really good friend/colleague; if you share what you are assessing they may contribute how different you appear to them at times.

Shared experience

In a workshop someone shared that gambling had become a larger part of her life. She mentioned that it was online and amounted to hours spent, as well as money she didn't have. She shared how she felt about it; used by others (sites) and missing other things in her life. At the same time, another girl spoke out about how she felt. She was a friend, and said that she had felt a distance had appeared between them. She knew that her friend was gambling but that was her business, but she missed her company.

The impact is twofold. Both are experiencing changes in the way that they feel as a result of this relationship. It was the case that she didn't really count the gambling on her phone as gambling. She told herself that it was on the phone, so not like going out and placing a bet. She was only spending little amounts, and this was thanks to the app which allowed the flexibility. She had convinced herself that it was a safe relationship.

The friend was asking herself questions like – why are we not spending time together? Is it something I've done, and am I missing out on something?

Exercise

On a sheet of paper, or a screen; place yourself in the middle. Draw circles around you that represent environments you inhabit – home, work, leisure places, clubs, meeting places with mates, any others you can think of. The size of the circle will represent the importance in meeting your needs/wants. Draw a line between yourself and the circle, the farther it extends away the less time you spend there.

How does it look to you?

Reflect on what people in certain circles see in the relationship. Does the length of the line equate to the importance that is assigned to it? When you look at the circles, think of the people and drugs that may be within it. Do they have an effect on the way you are assessing it?

It is important to look at you, your self and your relationships from a balanced perspective. There are associations in my life. They associate with me as well as I associate with them. We all have something to offer to another and relationships help us in our development.

Shared experience

Each of us is wonderfully created. We have gifts relating to kindness, caring, and we are relational so that we can share with others. We are always learning as we walk down our pathway, we are all participating in a journey and our paths cross. One body, many parts.

Summary

The relationship with ourselves is the most important as it informs our external relationships. We should listen to it and try to surround ourselves with care-givers in order to safeguard it.

When walking our pathway, we should look where we are going as there are places where we can trip. However, this is a learning process that provides experience that serves us well.

Exercise

Chapter Ten

The Self: Where my Pathway Leads

We have explored the nature of relationships, in terms of other people and drugs (substance and activity). At the same time it has been necessary to reflect on the self, and how an interaction with another impacts on us. How we respond in a relationship is influenced by the way we feel at any given moment. The content of what is said, what is inferred, what is suggested; is assessed against our current self.

Our self, our consciousness, reflects our state of being. As we move along our pathway and meet company, encounter traffic (sometimes heavy) in our environments; our self is coloured by our experiences. Any given current state can darken; and the underlying feeling, as we reflect on conversations and our interpretation, lead to negative thoughts. These negative thoughts can manifest themselves in a variety of reactions. We may contemplate a perceived threat, we may doubt our judgement, we may consider retaliation.

Alternatively, any given state can experience a lightening (lighten the mood). Our perception of what we have received, or experienced, may warm ourselves. Our inner state may suggest that we respond to others with positivity, and welcome company.

The situation is fluid and outcomes depend on the state of the relationship when we are participating. A relationship will, at various stages of growth, have its ups and downs. This is inevitable, for many of the reasons we have already covered. Which variables are in play when we are interacting with the other? For instance, there are two individuals here. There may be enough in common to engage both parties; possibly, a third the drug, or interest from others online. Are we both on the same page, is there difference of opinion on the direction the relationship is going? Is there someone new on the scene (a drug, like Winbig or Cookie monster), how does that change the dynamic? In addition, how do I feel? I have a private side as well as my public persona.

There is a constant internal referencing going on. Our instinct is involved, what is that telling us? Its role is primarily survival, the patrolling of our boundaries; what is acceptable and that we can deal with, and what is unacceptable, and needs to be defended against?

On the surface it appears that it is a long process where we need to remove ourselves and reflect. However, whether we are chatting on social media as part of a crowd, or responding to numerous posts, or just sitting in a park with a friend and chatting, there is a constant self-analysis taking place consisting of: how do I feel, what shall I say/do? I am getting out of here, or this is great, bring it on!

But what about the question of where I have been and where I am going? This is a question that we ask ourselves at various stages as we proceed down our pathway. We may be prompted by the breaking of a relationship that has left a vacuum; it may be age-related, sometimes illness that can lead to a depressed state, it varies. The question is part of the internal dialogue we have mentioned previously. When checking in, our self may prescribe a reset. We have spoken about how we are shaped through our experiences and our ambitions. The relationships we have, the company we interact with, both primary and secondary care-givers fill our memory with knowledge that informs our actions in the present and on the road ahead. On occasions we have pulled over and the reset is the option.

Puberty and menopause

An important junction that we all share an experience of is the onset and duration of puberty. Marked by age and changes we experience physically and psychologically, the step we make along our pathway, in this instance, is a stride. Similarly, the menopause will offer different challenges to individuals. These changes can present challenges to us. It is at these junctions in life that we need to have others that we trust to share our feelings. We hope to have primary care-givers, but there will probably be a range of types of relationships. Maybe there will be some that are similarly experiencing these life changes that we can listen to and speak with.

Reflections on past experience informing the present

In Chapter Three, we looked at an interview between someone removed from the situation (the interviewer) with a person and their chosen drug, with questions looking at how the relationship may develop for each of them.

Shared experience

Within the workshop, the interviewees are asked the same questions, you will recall. The idea is for the person to review the interaction from the start to looking into what the future may bring. In addition, they are invited to see the relationship from the other perspective.

It is generally accepted that you should "live in the moment"; that there is "nothing to be gained from looking back"; and that "who knows what tomorrow will bring". On the face of it this makes sense; however, we do look back.

The self contains memories and experiences from our past that inform some of our choices in the present. There is an element of safeguarding within that has been constructed; in addition, recalling where we have felt achievement and taken a big step forward along our pathway. You could say that you can recall where the potholes were that you dropped into and the freewheeling downhill sections.

The important aspect when we approach looking back is to make it a reflection. It's a little like casting your eye over from a distance; as opposed to dwelling upon it, that is returning and being there. It may be that falling into a pothole has been a learning curve. The fact that you got up with strength of will and strode forward indicates a measure of growth. This is a success, a good memory.

Shared experience

When in the prison, I had someone opposite me who stated that when he was ten he experienced his father leaving home; his mother reacting and taking it out on him, and subsequently withdrawing into himself. The reason that he had been leading a lifestyle of acquisitive crime was because he was entitled, and making up for what he had missed out on. If nobody was bothered to look after him and provide what he needed, he would take it for himself.

He was eighteen, and I asked how long he would be continuing to live his life stuck in 1998 (eight years earlier)? Whilst seeing how he might take this view, he now had opportunities to take another path.

This scenario was repeated frequently, you would present these thoughts when the person appeared to be dwelling, and we would discuss as a reflection to seek a way forward.

We also reflect, at times, on people and drugs that we have had a long-standing relationship with. Who are they? Why are we still growing individually and collectively? Clearly the present and the past is connected through some relationships and environments that we are comfortable in.

For example, we may have a long-standing relationship from school or university. This person has been a guide along our pathway although our routes may have parted at times. It has been the continuity and reliability that have held it together; the strength of which has enabled adversity to be overcome. A relationship with alcohol may be one that binds and divides. It may also be just someone who is present with others, sometimes in the background, sometimes the centre of attention. As already looked at, this drug, commonly seen as socially acceptable, has to be viewed from an individual's perspective. This normally means – how is my drinking affecting me and others in any particular environment such as, work, study and leisure?

A reflection on the past, in terms of relationships, can be considered a health check. How do I feel today and what do I look like in the mirror? Am I moving forward and is it with purpose? Am I comfortable and ready to meet challenge? This is honest dialogue with your self, that informs.

Where I am going? Whose company is supportive, loving, wise and with my best interests at heart? At the same time am I reciprocating with the same supportive output, and contributing to a healthy relationship? What does my destination look like, and how far down the road ahead am I looking? When we glimpse the future, we may not even be sure of what the next day will bring. We have to be realistic, as taking steps forward will always be accepting risk at some level. In order to safeguard oneself, we review the constants in our life: people, drugs, the environment and its suitability; the confidants, our trusted companions; and possible pitfalls, what our self is warning us of. What type of person am I seeking to be in relation to others around me round the next bend?

Summary

A dialogue with your self is a constant, as you interact within relationships. As your internal guide and reference point for your state of being; the conversation can allow for reflection.

Having been shaped, as we have grown, through our past experiences we also get a sense of how to act in the present and consider our next steps. It is important to continue to move forward and not to dwell upon past experiences. To reflect is to take the positive learning from the experiences; and to assess our journey so far.

Therefore, we do need to live in the present and watch our steps. There is a danger that, by looking too far down the road, we may stumble over something right in front of ourselves. However, through the support of relationships that share our desire for growth, we find freedom. We can feel more confident and able to express ourselves; confident of a strong foundation.

Questions

- Are you, in any way, living your life through the past; in terms of the relationships you seek and the environments you reside in?
- Would you find it useful to have a conversation with your self to assess where you are on your pathway; or, is there a guide that can give you a perspective?
- Is there any part of your daily life that has become too dominant, and that is starting to manage you?

Journal

Chapter Eleven

Conclusions

Throughout this book we have explored elements of the relationships in our lives.

The variables

Elements that impact on each other as we interact, and how that affects our individual journeys. We have seen the similarities that exist in our engagement with drugs and with people. In addition, the outcomes where a drug or drugs are introduced to a person-to-person relationship, and how dynamics may alter.

The elements we have described as variables. They have manifested themselves as: role models, the existence of peer pressure, mood changes in you or the other, environment types, and expressions of our self at any given moment. Our instincts may sense threat or opportunity. These variables will impact on the nature of relationships, and therefore on our progress down the pathway.

The company and traffic

Each of us travels down a pathway, where we have company and traffic. The company will consist of guides – care-givers and secondary care-givers. At the same time, a constant dialogue will take place with your self reflecting thoughts and feelings. The traffic consists of encounters with people and drugs that inhabit a variety of environments. We will be coloured by our experiences and the ups and downs (benefits and threats) of relationships will impact on who we are – our self. This, in turn, will shape our output to others, and thus the walk of daily life continues.

In walking forward along our pathway, each of us will consider the destination. As we grow, we develop a sense of what we wish to achieve.

The freedom and imprisonment

For many, a sense of freedom through self-expression, a confidence of who they are within society is sought. We have looked at how, because we present as different from each other, there is a need for a juxtaposition. Thus imprisonment has been discussed in the sense of confining oneself; the need being to safeguard while moving forward on your life journey.

What aspects of freedom and imprisonment are beneficial to your self?

Through the dramas we have witnessed the differing agendas brought to situations, and heard from the drug who may be the common denominator. You may well have identified with an environment, or an argument being made, or a character. By viewing the scenario from outside, like the drug, you can observe influences at play.

When looking at some relationships and environments, we see difficulties in managing the dialogue so that you benefit and remain safe. It is so often the case that your involvement becomes managed and you are no longer calling the shots.

The freedom that we are looking for may include self-control, a harmony within relationships, expressing of ideas and a feeling of independence. Throughout the book we have seen how certain environments and elements of relationships can compromise the individual; the outcomes may not meet those expectations. In addition we have also seen the advantages of routine, safety first, and the following of the herd; knowing that if all these people are thinking that way, or are doing this, then I can't go wrong.

The choices we make at junctions in the road are important. The memories we have built up through experiences and guidance from care-givers and other relationships, inform us. We have looked at a variety of different environments within home, work and leisure. For example, the bar, the party, the street, the park and at home; where we bring a perspective, an opinion, a desire to celebrate or lift ourselves. These environments can contain unexpected situations that may affect us.

Our instincts are there to provide guidance when faced with scenarios that are unexpected. We explored this in terms of "fight or flight", in the light of the changing face of modern society. We observe, through interaction with social media, a relationship unlike any other. Whether a resident or visitor, it is a house with many rooms and many voices. In some respects the environment always offers the unexpected.

How we react to shared information will differ from person to person.

How this medium of relationship differs is that when someone shares – who is sharing? We are aware that a person, or any number of people, may receive our message/post/image. So, is what we want to say compromised in any way; will our herd instinct kick in to safeguard ourselves, or will our post have a possibility to provoke? The element of control, that we have found helpful in other environments, can incur risk here.

When we look at freedom in respect of a destination along our pathway; how does social media involvement work? On the face of it our views, our self-expression finds a platform. There is inspiration from countless others who have stepped out, through this relationship, to express themselves and their own ideas. However, the nature of the company and the traffic generated can create different sensations. Each of us being different suggests that some may find the static overwhelming, possibly even threatening. There is a need to stay in touch with your self and seek the benefits of the relationship, and minimise the risks.

An important aspect is to recognise that we have a choice. A choice to get involved, to listen first, to state our own position: not only with social media, but with our approach to any environment. By being aware of how a relationship can change, as we interact with people and drugs, we can develop sound judgement.

Questions

+ Who is/are your guide(s): people, drugs, self?

Journal

Bonus Chapter

Fight, Flight or Film it

Scene

A man is walking through the town centre. He is talking to himself, and has an unkempt appearance. At the same time, a group of school children are walking on their way home from school. They see him, start to shout out comments and approach him. He stops, turns to them and shouts then moves on.

Several people have seen this scene, and filmed on their smartphones the man shouting.

Background

The man has mental-health issues that affect his social skills and manifest in a frequent dialogue with himself.

Consider how this scene, when posted, will be received.

Have you noticed a change in our response to threat? From prehistory, an inbred response has developed within mankind to initially survive, and then to evade danger. It is an instinct that still resides within us – "fight or flight". The change to our psyche, through our engagement with smartphone technology, has been to remain in the situation and film (video/photograph) the scene.

Fight or flight

We will be aware individually of how we react when we feel threatened. We have a sense of a possible confrontation, actions from those around us that suggests danger. How we interpret them is based on our age, and experience that has built up through witnessing danger.

In the young there may be a naivety from a protected environment; the instinct for survival not fully matured. In this case, a perceived threat will prompt adults to instinctively remove them from the scene. As we grow older and inevitably learn from experience, an assessment process automatically happens. This informs our action, but the fight or flight instinct also produces a reaction. It may be that physique contributes to a decision – do we err on the side of caution or are we of a mind to confront? For example, someone who has previously faced a threat, taken time to weigh up the risk and decided to intervene. In this scenario it may be that the man or woman has a background in work that has trained them to assess situations and tackle the threat in a decisive but safe way.

Ordinarily though, for many of us, when our senses raise an awareness of danger, the fight or flight instinct activates. Those that choose fight may see others demonstrate that they are going to confront the situation. Within the seconds that decisions are made, this weighs the balance in terms of getting involved. An example can be where many gather together in a protest situation. Some of the gathering will attend with a strong conviction to make a statement, and a number decide to increase the level of confrontation. In this instance, others may feel impelled to join in, and others continue with a presence but do not heighten their involvement.

We are relational and have a herd mentality. The fight or flight instinct includes this factor in our reasoning. These instinctive steps forwards or backwards are not considered reflection but a rapid assessment; something clicks in the psyche triggered by the environment.

Most of the reaction is born out of a sense, an intuition that originates from within us. Have you been in a situation in a crowded bar, pub, club or party where, without any direct argument that you are aware of, the atmosphere changes? You look around and everyone appears to have felt the same. Many journalists working in the field would tell you that they have a nose for a story or a picture; this would appear to be instinctual. Their role does demand film it! But in reality it is fight, getting involved in order to seize the moment.

The alternative flight instinct, again is instinctual and is a choice based on a multitude of reasons. Some are more obvious and convincing to the person than others. We may find ourselves in an overwhelming situation. There could be an immediate and clear risk to life, where no one would contemplate stepping into it. To flee is the obvious move to make, and even those professionals who can assess what's happening will do so. The response that many will make will be driven by the need to protect. Our care for others that are vulnerable (age, health constraints) can take over and shielding is offered in flight.

We do have to acknowledge that some of us may not be able to overcome a sense of self-preservation, and act accordingly. It may be the case that we start moving away while, at the same time, our mind is telling us the opposite. We can be scared of what is happening, fearful of what may happen next. We may reproach ourselves later, but this can be a force over which we have no control in that instant.

In addition, a place of safety may be pointed out and the sensible course of action is to make for it. At the same time, our thinking will be that others will know it too; this will comfort us as we turn away.

As we look at the reasoning behind the fight or flight alternatives for each of us; there must be an understanding that it is in a moment, and when faced with that moment we immediately search within ourselves. There are things happening around us, communications and actions, but what we do is based on the remembered information from the past; recalled words remembered from care-givers, merged into a response.

Film it

Is it really possible that a relatively new phenomenon, the modern phone, has become an integral part of our instinctual make-up? One thing that we can't ignore is that whenever there is a situation that suggests threat, or where danger is actually existent and affecting people; there are phones recording or photographing.

The fact that images are being made and reproduced in media situations is commonplace. Through a multitude of communication channels, situations that create interest are being filmed. The events can be of any interest; attention-grabbing for lots of reasons. The herd instinct takes over automatically as where one phone goes up, others follow. The evidence is seen online and footage makes its way onto universal platforms. Many reports on events covered by the news include coverage including that supplied from a phone. In addition, authorities such as the police will actively seek images originating from personal phones to provide evidence of a situation.

Why are people choosing to film it? There are many facets of this, to look at. Initially we need to examine if people who film actually have a choice. You may say that, of course, they can just not do so. Many may just look at what has caught the attention of others, stand and watch, and then move on. Of course, bearing in mind what we have already spoken about the standing and watching may be replaced by the instinctual assessment demanded by fight or flight. This is the area that needs to be examined with regard to the filming of a situation that could endanger.

Firstly, we have to acknowledge that the phone use, regardless of the situation, is an automatic reflex for many. It is a fact that the phone is in hand and for the resident, part of the hand. Thus its use, which has increasingly been around the camera, is normal behaviour. Now we do need to add that the relationship people have with their phone differs with each person. As we have spoken about already, how often and how long the use of the phone occurs depends, to a large extent, on the individual's natural state of being. If our natural state is to interact all of the time when possible, then it's not a question of a choice debated. With this state people live in a kind of bubble; in this respect, someone may become unaware of what is occurring around them. How this manifests itself is that the individual will recognise the environment and what is happening; however, it may be the case that they are not tuned in to their instinctive feelings. We can become habitual within our interaction with the phone, with a continual checking in. Therefore, an automatic, reflex-like action kicks in. This interaction is a behaviour that becomes normal (instinct); so how does this sit alongside fight or flight?

Has film it materialised alongside the present inbred responses? Is it the case that the instinctual assessment that occurs as previously described, also includes reaching for the phone?

It might appear that three options are weighed up and film it is a recognised choice. Now whether it is an instinctual choice when faced with threat, or not: is it reasonable to assume that, dependent on the relationship and its addictive aspect, it can override the others? What are the ramifications of this?

We should also not neglect to mention other reasoning why people may choose to film/photo-post. Aside from the discussion around internal response, is there an aspect of making a comment? Depending on the nature of the situation, we can use the phone to state an opinion: "I think that this needs to be highlighted because I think that . . . "; "this needs to be seen by others". It may be a tragedy, an unprovoked attack, a beautiful event/scene; alternatively, it may be something that needs to be revealed, I need to report this. "I have the means at my disposal to inform the widest possible audience on what I am experiencing, and to express the way that I am feeling."

Concerns

So far, we have explored the nature of the phenomenon of almost constant interaction between person and phone, in the context of fight, flight or film it. The fact that, as individuals, we all have a different relationship with the phone, can sometimes be overridden by the herd mentality and also the person that we are.

The amount and the severity of threat of danger in places that we live hasn't changed. In fact, it can be argued that the nature of danger and the extremity of it has increased. The inbred response still exists and probably saves lives, certainly serves us well today. We have also had to adapt to different types of threat; where getting away from a situation has created challenges that are testing. The fight response has also changed in nature. It is well known that this response can bring risks. The concerns that are known are compromising the safety of the general public, the emergency services, and post-situation investigation. In a street scenario, where an accident occurs, sometimes things just happen. Some people, as we have already discussed, will, through natural instinct, step into it. How this turns out will go one of two ways, personally and for others. Where instinctively someone stays (maybe draws closer) and films, it is likely that there is a heightened risk of the same order. There may be a risk in the ways set out, this reaction is neither forward or backward. Each person has to make their own judgement in relation to their actions.

There is another angle to be taken into account with regard to the filming it. It is about the choice of posting it and to whom? The nature of filming can instigate a chain reaction if posted. This may be the intention of the individual; to share, encourage comment, maybe even provoke reaction. The initial action, when in the moment, is to film. The situation will, when seen, relate or not relate to those receiving. If it does, how is the post received?

A chain reaction of response and action can be triggered. This, of course, may have been the intention; however, there is another area to look at here. An image or a clip are interpreted in a moment by the user, there is a reason why they are taken by her/him, a group. When people receive, they do so in a different context that is not present; their state is not impacted upon by the situation viewed. So, what does this mean? There is a contrast between the reality (of a situation) and an image seen without a context. How this plays out, in terms of reaction, will vary.

The point is that whether you consider that film it has become part of an instinctive response when faced with threat or danger; or is a habitual action by many for whatever response, it happens.

Summary

The phone has become indispensable to many. Where we see its use in public situations containing risk of danger, we might consider that its use has claimed a part of our natural-response mechanism. To some it may be a choice to express an interest in what is happening; others may feel the need to share.

We need to be aware that as with fight or flight, there may be consequences that we are unable to foresee.

Questions

- Do you feel that your filming, if you do, is habitual or an instinct? Can you choose?
- Is it your tendency to comment/follow when you see certain posts?
- Do you think that people place themselves at unnecessary risk when filming these scenarios?

Journal

Glossary

Drug – something that alters your state of mindsets.

Freedom – the power or right to act, speak or think as one wants; the state of not being imprisoned.

Junctions – when we arrive at a place where we are presented with "should I choose this way or that way?" It may be an internal dialogue with your self, taking into account instinct, or advice from a guide. Alternatively, arriving at a lot of traffic on your pathway – pressure from social media, where the choice is get involved or leave alone?

Pathway – the journey that we take, each different; although sometimes it appears that we are sharing with many.

Reset – an internal conversation, or with a trusted and empathic other. A consideration of recent steps taken and whether you have received what you needed from a relationship, or a course of action. Have you been damaged or is the path ahead a risk with little or no reward? "What are the choices I have?"

Shared experience – reflections on experiences from my working life that have contributed to what has been shared in this chapter.

Static – mass traffic on the pathway, can be confusing, threatening, as well as informing and supportive. The user has to be aware of how, what is communicated, can be difficult to receive and respond to. The static contains many opinions and many expressions of them.

Traffic – those that we encounter, by choice or otherwise; they may become company, can be singular entity/person (a drug), or a number of people (and drugs).

Variables – factors that can impact on a relationship at any given time. Mood change, the other changing during the relationship, external influence such as peer pressure. Feelings internally that make us think differently about a situation, boundaries being pushed – realisation that this is not what I want.

Lightning Source UK Ltd.
Milton Keynes UK
UKHW020730270522
403617UK00011B/643